CRIMINAL COLD CASES

CRIMINAL COLD CASES

FUGITIVES FINALLY BROUGHT TO JUSTICE

CHARLOTTE GREIG

ARCTURUS

ARCTURUS
This edition published in 2011 by Arcturus Publishing Limited
26/27 Bickels Yard, 151–153 Bermondsey Street,
London SE1 3HA

ISBN: 978-1-84837-121-7
AD000182EN

Printed in Singapore

Images reproduced with the permission of the following:

Corbis: 15, 17, 27, 29, 30, 47, 59, 63, 64, 67, 75, 77, 79, 89, 90, 93, 94, 107, 121, 122, 131, 143, 151, 152, 161, 167, 175, 178, 201, 202, 206
Empics: 19, 20, 23, 33, 35, 36, 41, 42, 45, 49, 50, 53, 54, 57, 66, 81, 83, 84, 97, 98, 101, 103, 105, 111, 112, 114, 149, 183, 184, 186, 189, 190, 192, 195, 199
Getty: 76, 117, 125
Shutterstock: 137, 138, 155, 156, 177 and all page montage images
Austin Police Dept Homicide Cold Case Unit: 143, 144
Ben Rosengart <http://narcissus.net/>: 69
Jeffrey Bayer/Clifford Jeffreys, New Jersey State Dept of Corrections: 206
Pima County Sheriff's Dept: 196
Thanks to Kevin Green and the Innocence Project: 171
Thanks to the Twells family: 205
University of Tennessee/Video and Photography Center: 138
Wichita County Sheriff's Office: 165

With thanks to Stacy Horn for her book *The Restless Sleep: Inside New York City's Cold Case Squad* (Transworld 2005), used as a reference source for this book.

CONTENTS

INTRODUCTION

TODAY, IN THE WORLD'S CITIES, THERE ARE HUNDREDS OF COLD CASES ON THE FILES OF POLICE DEPARTMENTS. THESE ARE THE CASES THAT HAVE GONE UNSOLVED FOR YEARS: CASES WHERE, PERHAPS, THERE WERE NO LEADS; WHERE CLUES THAT SEEMED PROMISING AT FIRST LED NOWHERE; WHERE EVIDENCE WAS LOST, OR WENT UNNOTICED; WHERE, FOR WHATEVER REASON, WITNESSES WOULD NOT COME FORWARD.

Sometimes, according to the nature of the case, there may have been intense pressure at the time from the local community, the media, and the public in general, to solve the crime; in other instances, nobody cared about the victims, and the crime was not reported in the newspapers or on TV until many years later.

Whatever the circumstances, the police usually make every effort to find the perpetrators of serious crimes as quickly as possible; but of course, as in all other walks of life, mistakes are made and bureaucratic systems cause delay. The element of human error also plays a part, whether it is sheer incompetence or emotional bias of some kind. All these factors lead to the same outcome: a file that sits on the shelves of the police department, gathering dust over the years until it has been forgotten.

Yet, in recent years, a growing number of cold cases have been taken down

off the shelves, dusted off, reviewed, and finally solved – often years, decades even, after the crimes were committed. This book tells the fascinating story of those cases. Here are stories of killers who were tracked down after years of believing that they had, literally, got away with murder. Some of them are famous: for example, Dennis Rader, better known as 'BTK', the serial killer who signed his taunting letters with the initials that stood for 'Bind, Torture, Kill', his horrifying method of murder; or Gary Leon Ridgeway, aka The Green River Killer, who was finally tracked down after many years, and is now thought to be America's most prolific serial killer ever. Other killers are less well known, but no less evil: Danny Keith Hooks, who murdered five prostitutes in a crack house; or Joe Clark, a psychotic teenager who liked to break the bones of younger boys before putting them to death. They, like the others, escaped justice for a long time but, finally, the long arm of the law reached out to them.

Victims' stories

The book also tells the story of the victims, as well as the killers: young women like Martha Moxley, whose murder took decades to solve before it was found that the murderer was a young, privileged teenager like herself, living in the gated community of the super-rich at Belle Haven, Connecticut. Or Jill Dando, the British TV personality who was shot dead in an execution-style killing outside her house in a quiet London street. The circumstances of her killing led detectives to believe for a time that it had been politically motivated, but as it transpired, the explanation was simpler than that. She was murdered – like so many other female victims – by a mentally disturbed, obsessive loner. Similarly, the case of Hilda Murrell, an elderly woman living in the English countryside, caused a political storm when it was suggested that her death was a result of skulduggery among high-ranking figures in the British political elite; however, once again, there was less to the case than met the eye – her killer turned out to be an armed robber with no political connections whatsoever.

DNA profiling

Most of the cold cases described in this book were solved by a relatively new method, which has proved more effective than any other in recent years: DNA profiling. Today, in most American states, convicted felons are required to give DNA samples to the police, usually as mouth swabs. Data on these samples is fed into a national database, which is growing ever more extensive as every year passes. Meanwhile, evidence from unsolved past cases, such as blood, semen, and hair samples found on the bodies of victims, are used to make a DNA profile of the perpetrator of the crime. These profiles are fed into the computer and checked against the database.

Reliability

The evidence taken from DNA profiles is extremely reliable: unless it can be proved that samples have been tampered with in some way, there can be no doubt that a DNA match is conclusive. This is because every single individual in the world has their own unique DNA. Moreover, unlike other methods, such as fingerprinting, DNA does not degrade or wear out over time. A sample taken from a corpse many years ago yields the same results as one taken just a few days before. For these reasons, DNA profiling is the single most powerful tool in solving the many cold cases on America's police department files today. And this looks set to continue. Theoretically, at least, it seems that hundreds of cases could be solved in this way: by matching the DNA profile of an individual on the database to that of samples taken from a victim's body – as long as evidence containing DNA was kept by the detective team at the time.

Of course, the system is not foolproof. There are many killers who are not on a police database, so that even if their DNA code is known, there is no way of tracing them. Only by matching their code with that of convicted felons on the database can the police track down a murderer. And, of course, not everyone who commits murder, even serial murder, is on the police's books. But sooner or

later, most of these crazed individuals come into contact with the law, in some way or other – be it only for a small matter such as a speeding fine; and when they do, they find that their past catches up with them, in no uncertain terms.

Other methods to solve cold cases

Crucial as it has proved to be in recent years – and promises to be in the future – DNA profiling is not the only method that solves cold cases. All across America, there are now specialist units that employ a variety of approaches to solve these difficult crimes. These include the work of Frank Bender, a forensic sculptor. Instead of issuing a sketch of the suspect, police go to Bender, who creates a bust instead. Liaising with detectives, a psychologist, and others, Bender uses his uncanny ability to visualize the appearance of an individual. He uses clues from the killer's life, analysing his daily routines, his likes and dislikes, and so on, to build up a picture of what he would look like today. One of Bender's greatest triumphs was the case of John List, the oldest, coldest case that had ever appeared on the TV show, *America's Most Wanted*. List had disappeared after murdering his entire family, and had been in hiding for decades. It was up to Bender to imagine how he had aged during that period of time, and how he might have tried to disguise his identity. To the surprise of all concerned, Bender managed to get every detail of his image of List exactly right, even down to the glasses the killer was wearing when he was arrested.

Other unusual methods of solving cold cases includes the work of Dr William Bass at The Body Farm, the nickname of the Anthropology Research Facility at the University of Tennessee. Essentially, Bass studies the way insects act on decomposing human bodies, using real corpses donated to the facility. He measures the length of maggots, times the breeding cycles of various insects, studies how they prey on the carcass and on each other, studies meteorological information for the period in question, all to one end – to find out the exact date and time that the victim died. This, in many instances, gives police vital

information as to the circumstances of the murder – information that, often, would have been impossible to gain in any other way.

Necrosearch is another crime-solving unit that brings together the skills of many specialists, from geologists and botanists to anthropologists and meteorologists, to analyze what they call 'clandestine gravesites' – that is, bodies that have been secretly buried, often in remote places. Working together, the group make a grid of the area where a suspected victim lies buried, and conduct a methodical search over the terrain, picking up clues as to soil, animal and plant irregularities as they go, and noting other changes. In this way, they have managed to assist the police in several cases, including that of Michelle Wallace, a young hiker who was murdered and then buried in a remote area of Gunnison, Colorado, in 1974. Attempts to find her murderer failed at the time, but eighteen years later, the case was reopened and Necrosearch, using their combined skills, managed to locate her grave. Her killer, who had been picked up by police and let go shortly after the crime, because of lack of evidence, was re-arrested and this time, charged with murder. He was later convicted and given a life sentence.

Detective work

However, cold cases are not always solved with the help of the latest advances in science and technology. A lot of case-solving still relies, as it always has, on good old-fashioned police work. In modern times, as well as in the past, cases have often been solved after years of dogged enquiry by a single detective who refuses to give up until his work is done. For example, it was only through the persistence of one detective, William King, that the notorious serial child-murderer and cannibal Albert Fish was finally caught and put to death in 1936, after decades of eluding the police. Through a combination of sharp-eyed observational skills and untiring determination to catch his man, King managed to trace a taunting letter that Fish had sent to the mother of one of his victims, Grace Budd. He eventually found Fish in a cheap New York boarding house, and at last

came face to face with the monster he had been chasing for so many years: a small, grey-haired man who was quietly sipping tea with his landlady. Fish jumped up and attacked King with a razor, but King overpowered him. Fish was later convicted in a sensational trial, and sent to the electric chair.

Cases such as that of Albert Fish are truly horrifying, but this book describes those in which moral decency, as well as evil, plays a part. Many cold cases are solved when witnesses, who may have been silent for many years, finally feel a call of conscience and step forward to tell their story. This is what happened in the case of Rose Twells, an elderly widow who was brutally robbed and murdered in 1979 by a group of young men: Jeffrey Bayer, Clifford Jeffrey, and Mark English. It was not until 1993 that Luanne Waller, Bayer's former girlfriend, approached the police and told them her story. She said that she had been told to keep watch while the boys entered the house, and that after they came out they had bragged about murdering the old lady. Waller's story was corroborated by another witness who then stepped forward, Shirley Logan, who had been dating Clifford Jeffrey at the time. As a result of their evidence, Bayer, Jeffrey, and English were charged with murder, and Bayer convicted.

Finally, we come to the cold cases which are, perhaps, most significant of all: those which have been solved after many years, not just because of an individual's call of conscience, but because of society's need to see justice done. In this category are the famous civil rights cases of Medgar Evers, the Freedom Riders, and the Birmingham church bombings. Through the solving of these cases, where innocent black people were murdered and their white, racist killers allowed to go free, we see how racial injustice – indeed, an entire culture of lawlessness in the American South – has come to be viewed in the present day as an issue that must be addressed. And with the civil rights cases, as with all the cold cases described in this book, we also see how important it is, not just for the relatives of the victim concerned, but for society as a whole, to continue to solve these crimes – however long the road to justice may be.

911
ALERT
Treasurer of the United States

IN COLD BLOOD

Murder is always shocking, but there are certain murders that seem, for whatever reason, to be more lurid than most. These are the cold cases where it is the crime, not the killer, that remains in the public imagination.

The Crack House Murders is a sordid tale in which addict Danny Keith Hooks killed five women in a crack house where women came to sell sex for drugs, after apparently attempting to involve them in an orgy. His crime went undetected for five years, but eventually he was picked up for rape, and his DNA profile was found to match that of samples recovered from the scene of the crime. In the case of the Lady in the Lake, victim Carol Park's relatives had to wait twenty-one years before finding out what happened to her. Her body was found by scuba divers in Coniston Water, a beauty spot in the north of England, which eventually led to the conviction of her ex-husband, Gordon, for her murder.

The Bone Breaker is the tale of a deranged teenager, Joe Clark, who enjoyed hearing his victims' bones break before killing them; it was only when one of his victims escaped that he was caught and put behind bars. In the Slaughter of the Innocents, we look at the Schuessler-Peterson case, in which three young boys were brutally murdered after an innocent trip to the cinema in Chicago; here, the murderer Kenneth Hansen was brought to book after several of his ex-lovers and friends testified against him. Finally, we investigate the bizarre case of the Woman in the Box, in which victim Carol Smith was kept captive as a slave for seven and a half years by a couple named Janice and Cameron Hooker. She was only rescued when Janice Hooker became jealous of her, and tipped off the police.

01

DANNY KEITH HOOKS: THE CRACK HOUSE MURDERS

ONE OF THE MOST SHOCKING MULTIPLE MURDERS TO OCCUR IN THE 1990S WAS THAT OF FIVE BLACK WOMEN, WHO WERE STABBED TO DEATH IN A CRACK HOUSE IN THE NORTH-EAST AREA OF OKLAHOMA CITY. THE MURDERS OCCURRED IN 1992, BUT IT WAS NOT UNTIL FIVE YEARS LATER THAT THE AUTHORITIES CAUGHT UP WITH THE PERPETRATOR, WHO HAD MANAGED TO STEER CLEAR OF THE LAW, EVADING ALL RESPONSIBILITY FOR SUCH A TERRIBLE CRIME UP UNTIL THAT TIME.

On 16 May 1992, police were called to a crack house to find a horrifying scene. It was one of carnage: five women lay dead, butchered by an unknown assailant. They were all found naked, lying in pools of blood; and four of the victims were also found to have been sexually assaulted. The victims were 47-year-old Phyllis Adams, 35-year-old Sandra Thompson, 37-year-old Carolyn Watson, 30-year-old LaShawn Evans, and 34-year-old Fransill Roberts.

Butchered in a crack house

Samples of blood were taken from some of the women's clothing, including two shirts and a jacket, as well as a bloody handprint that was found on a curtain. However, the murder investigation launched at the time yielded no results, and no

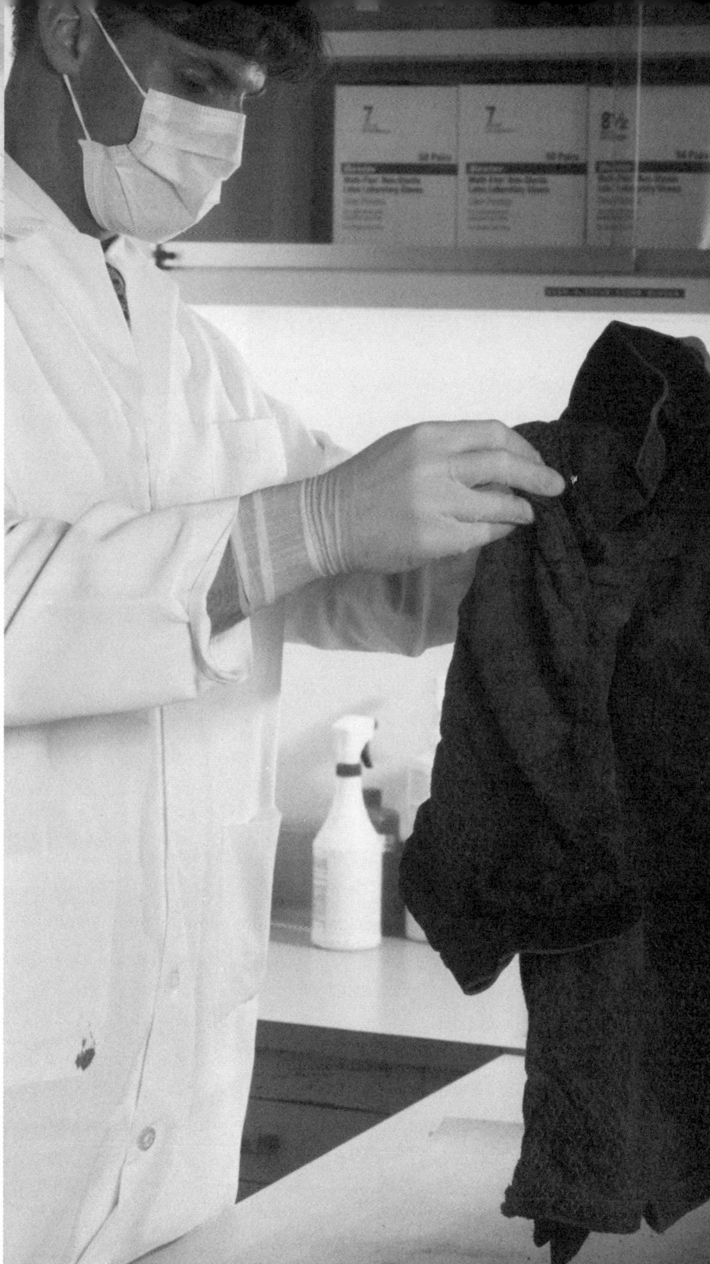

Storing DNA profiles: people who have committed crimes in earlier years now stand a very good chance of being linked to their past if they offend again, thanks to DNA evidence

suspect was named. The multiple murders shocked the local community, and the police were criticized for failing to find the killer. The National Association for the Advancement of Colored People (NAACP) accused the law enforcement agencies of racism, saying they were not making enough effort to find the culprit because the victims were black and were frequenting a crack house. (The house was known as a place where penniless drug addicts, mostly women, came to sell sex in return for drugs.) Many commentators from the black community felt that because of the house's bad reputation, very little was being done to bring the killer of these women to justice.

It was not until five years later that police ran the DNA profile of Danny Keith Hooks into their computer database. Hooks had been picked up on a charge of rape. To their surprise, it matched the samples taken from the scene of the crime at the crack house. The evidence was compelling, and Hooks was soon brought to trial and charged with the five murders.

At the trial, Hooks claimed that the bloody handprint on the curtain was the result of a cut on his hand that he had sustained from riding his bicycle. He admitted that he had smoked crack at the house earlier that day with the five women, and that he had had sex with two of them. However, he said that he had then decided to leave the house and it was only when he returned later that he had found the dead bodies.

The prosecution alleged that to the contrary, Hooks had killed the women in a frenzy of violence. He was a crack addict who had become mentally unstable as a result of his addiction, and had tried to force the women into a sex orgy with him. When they had refused and tried to leave, he had attacked them, killing all five women.

Death penalty

The jury in the case deliberated for fourteen hours, over a period of two days. What held their deliberation up was the fact that it was hard to understand how

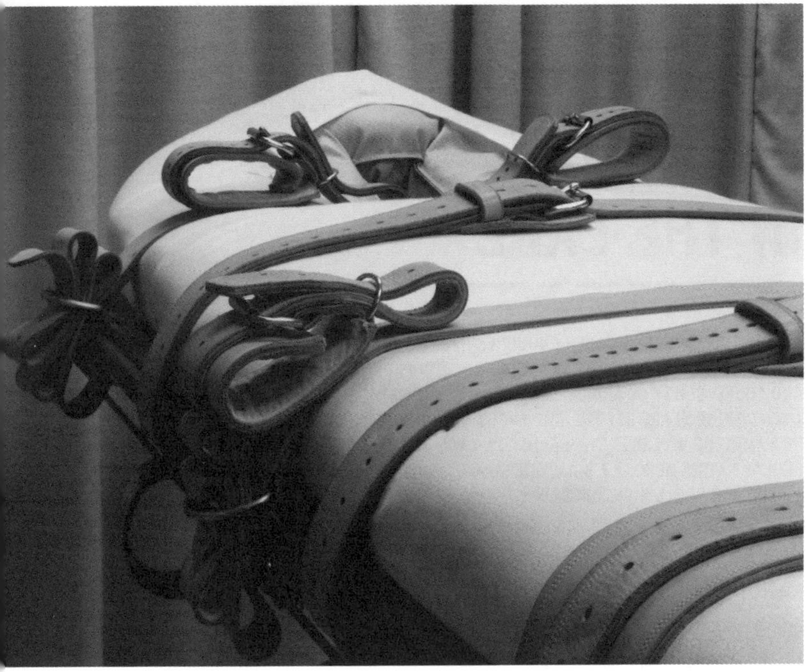

Guilty: Danny Keith Hooks received five separate death sentences for the murders

five women could have been killed – apparently easily – by one man, but in the end they decided that that was what had happened. They therefore returned a verdict of guilty. On hearing the verdict, Hooks showed no reaction. He was convicted of five counts of first-degree murder and sentenced to death. Commenting on the death penalty for Hooks, the daughter of victim Phyllis Adams, Barbara Booker, said 'I don't think he deserves to live because those women did not have a choice'.

GORDON PARK: THE LADY IN THE LAKE

ONE OF THE LONGEST MURDER ENQUIRIES EVER TO TAKE PLACE IN THE UNITED KINGDOM WAS FINALLY RESOLVED WHEN GORDON PARK WAS BROUGHT TO TRIAL AND FOUND GUILTY OF MURDERING HIS WIFE. THE CRIME HAD HAPPENED TWENTY-NINE YEARS BEFORE, AND MIGHT NEVER HAVE BEEN DISCOVERED HAD NOT AMATEUR DIVERS IN THE BEAUTIFUL LAKE DISTRICT OF THE NORTH OF ENGLAND COME ACROSS A BODY ONE SUMMER'S DAY: THE BODY OF A WOMAN IN A BLUE BABY-DOLL NIGHTDRESS.

The 'mystery lover'

Gordon Park and his wife Carol were teachers. They were a successful couple, living what seemed from the outside like a happy, settled life. Gordon had built the family home himself. But all was not as it seemed, and those who knew the couple well realized there were problems in the marriage. According to Gordon, when they first married they were deliriously happy – he described their relationship as 'love's young dream'. However, as his defence lawyer later pointed out when describing the relationship in court, trouble then began to surface as Carol – described as 'vivacious and attractive' – took to having affairs quite openly. On two occasions, she left her husband to live with her lovers. Yet Park was understanding about his wife's behaviour. Although upset by her dalliances, he made a great deal of effort to be open-minded and let his wife

Gordon Park lived a full life – something he denied his wife when he bludgeoned her to death with an ice axe before dumping her body in a lake

have her freedom. The defence stressed that the relationship had not been an abusive one, and that Park had hoped that he and his wife could have a peaceful 'open marriage'. As the lawyer put it, Park had 'put up with a great deal' from his wife, and had behaved in a restrained way as far as was humanly possible.

However, by 1976, the couple's relationship had deteriorated and was unstable. By this time, both Gordon and Carol Park were involved with other partners, and it was not uncommon for them to spend weeks apart.

On the day Carol disappeared, 17 July 1976, the family had planned a trip to the seaside resort of Blackpool, but at the last minute Carol had said she felt ill, and had stayed at home. When the family returned home, Carol was not there. Gordon reported her absence to the police – but only after six weeks. Naturally enough, this caused suspicion, but Gordon told the police of his wife's affairs and said that he thought she had left him, taking off with a 'mystery lover'.

The body in the lake

The police conducted an investigation, but it was only a routine operation. Carol Park was filed as a missing person. No one suspected that Gordon had killed his wife, even though he issued no emotional appeals through the media for her to come back to him. He seemed unperturbed about her disappearance, but this was put down to the fact that the couple's relationship had deteriorated in recent years. Speaking later at Park's trial, Detective Chief Inspector Keith Churchman, who took over the investigation in 2001, commented that he and his officers had done everything they could to find Carol, but that the enquiry was conducted as a 'missing persons' incident, not a murder case, and that they had very little to go on as a result.

A happy family – but Carol Park had a string of affairs, leaving her husband and children on two occasions to live with lovers

And there the mystery might have remained, had not the body of Carol Park been found, by pure chance, twenty-one years later. In August 1997, a small group of amateur scuba divers was exploring a part of Coniston Water in the Lake District. This was a part of the lake that people usually avoided swimming in, because the water was so murky there. They swam far out from shore, and dived down eighty feet below the surface of the water. There, they unwittingly discovered a body resting on an underwater shelf. It was that of a woman, still wearing the blue baby-doll nightdress she had been killed in.

The body was later identified as that of Carol Park, and when the story hit the headlines, she was dubbed 'the lady of the lake'.

If the body had been thrown in the lake a little further away from the shore, it would have sunk to the bottom of the lake and would almost certainly never have been found. And Gordon Park would have got away with murder. As it was, the divers reported their finding to the police, who went straight round to Park's house. When they called, however, he was away on a cycling holiday in France with his third wife, Jenny. The house and his boat were searched for clues, and when Park returned, he was immediately arrested on a murder charge, and taken into custody.

However, the police were thwarted when the legal authorities decided that there was not evidence to bring the case to court. Park was let go, but the case remained open.

Bludgeoned to death

Four years later, the case of the 'lady in the lake', as it had now become known, was taken over by Chief Inspector Churchman. Churchman decided to review the investigation, going all the way back to 1976, to see if new clues could be uncovered. In the process, he managed to turn up new evidence. This time, it was found that the stones that had been attached to Carol Park's body to weigh it down in the water were the same kind used in the building of Gordon Park's house. Not only this, but a fellow prisoner who had spent time with Park while he was in police custody, Michael Wainwright, now contacted the police with new information. He said that while on remand in Preston prison, Park had confessed to him that he had murdered his wife.

There now seemed to be enough evidence to bring charges against Gordon Park, and this time when the police went back to the legal authorities to press for a court case, they were successful. In January 2004, Park was arrested again, and charged with the murder of his wife twenty-nine years before.

The ten-week trial attracted a great deal of attention from the media. As the prosecutor in the case pointed out to the jury, this was not a cut-and-dried case. Park could not be convicted on a single piece of evidence. On the contrary, there were many different pieces of evidence, but when they were all put together, they pointed to Park's guilt. In the context of this new evidence, Park's story about his wife leaving home with a 'mystery lover' looked flimsy, to say the least. Why had she never returned home once the fling was over, as she had before? And why had she never contacted her children, even after decades? These were questions that could not be answered except by one theory: that Park had murdered his wife and tried to cover his tracks.

The prosecution alleged on 17 July 1976 Park had brutally battered his wife to death with an ice axe. He had then wrapped her body in the nightdress she was wearing. Trussed up, he had put her body into several bags and then hauled it out into his car. He had driven to a deserted part of the Lake District, Coniston Water, transferred the body to his boat, rowed out far into the lake and thrown the body overboard. As it turned out, of course, he did not row out quite far enough.

A trance-like state

The jury believed the prosecution's story and, after a ten-week trial at Manchester Crown Court, Park was found guilty. Evidently, the fact that Park had had 'a lot to put up with' as a result of his wife's infidelities did not, in the jury's eyes, constitute a defence for battering her to death in her nightdress and throwing her body in the lake.

When he heard the verdict, Park looked stunned, and began to blink repeatedly, while a piercing shriek erupted from the public gallery. Park's wife, Jenny, began to sob as he was led away, still dazed and disoriented. It seemed that Park had never expected to be convicted after so long – before the verdict, he had told reporters that he expected to be released, and would be back soon to give interviews about his experience.

The judge sentenced him to life in prison, and told him that he must serve at least fifteen years before being considered for parole. He was not convinced that Park had conducted the murder in a premeditated manner, but he felt the degree of violence he had exhibited, as well as his cold-blooded disposal of the body, and his covering up of the murder for so many years, causing untold grief and anxiety to his wife's family, warranted an extremely long prison sentence.

Carol Park was described by her husband as 'attractive and vivacious' – qualities that would prove to be her downfall

Park was apparently pole-axed by the verdict. He was led from the court room in a trance-like state, holding out his hands in front of him and grasping a handrail for support. It was as though he could not believe that, after all this time, his crime had been discovered and that he would now have to pay the penalty for it. Today, he still maintains that he is innocent.

The body of the 'lady in the lake' tells a different story, however. Gordon Park thought that he had committed the perfect murder, and had managed to keep his secret safe for twenty-one years. But, by an extraordinary twist of fate, the body of his wife was dredged up from the depths of the lake where he had tried to hide it decades before. Thus it was that 'the lady in the lake' returned to haunt her husband, and Gordon Park, a quiet, retired school master, was finally brought to justice.

JOE CLARK: THE BONE BREAKER

NOBODY WANTS TO DIG UP A BODY - ESPECIALLY THE BODY OF SOMEONE WHO HAS DIED AS THE RESULT OF A TRAGIC ACCIDENT, AND WHOM RELATIVES FEEL SHOULD BE LEFT TO REST IN PEACE. YET IN SOME CASES, AFTER SUCH AN ACCIDENT - SOMETIMES YEARS LATER - DOUBTS BEGIN TO BE RAISED AS TO HOW EXACTLY THE VICTIM MET THEIR DEATH.

In these cases, the body must be dug up and looked at once again, this time more carefully. This is what happened in the dramatic case of Chris Steiner, a fourteen-year-old boy who was presumed drowned simply through a tragic accident, and who lay in his grave for a year before the authorities learned that his death may have been a violent one, and decided to investigate further.

Manner of death: undetermined

Chris Steiner lived in Baraboo, Wisconsin, and on the night of 4 July 1994, disappeared from his home. It was a mystery as to why he had disappeared; his parents could give no reason for it, and could not believe that he had simply run away from home. When the police were called in, they noticed sinister indications at the scene of the crime. It was clear that Chris' bedroom window had been

wrenched open, and there were muddy footprints on the carpet of the room, which suggested that someone had come in from outside and abducted the boy. Downstairs, a patio door was found to be unlocked, and it was thought that the intruder had entered the house through this door. A search was launched, but it was only six days later that the teenager's body was found. It was lying over a tree beside a sandbar on the Wisconsin River.

The quiet, peaceful community of Baraboo was shocked by this horrific, unexpected discovery. An autopsy on the body was performed, but the coroner could not say what had caused the boy's death. There was no sign that Steiner had been attacked or wounded. He had not been strangled. His body was bloated from being in the water, and thus his cause of death was listed as drowning. However, the coroner could not ascertain the manner of his death which meant that this could not be classified and his death was listed as undetermined.

Despite the circumstances of Steiner's disappearance, and the signs that he had been abducted from his home, the police were unable to make any headway in the subsequent investigation. Without any clear leads to follow, the case soon went cold.

Liked to hear bones break

It was only when the murderer struck again, and this time the victim escaped, that Chris Steiner's death was re-investigated. A year had passed when, on 29 July 1995, another boy from the area, thirteen-year-old Thad Phillips, was abducted from his home, this time in the early hours of the morning. Thad had been fast asleep on the living room couch when he woke to find himself being carried through the house. At first he thought it was one of his parents who had picked him up to take him to his bed. However, instead, the person took him outside. Still half asleep, Thad thought that he recognized the person as a friend of the family.

The abductor was Joe Clark, a seventeen-year-old young man who lived in the

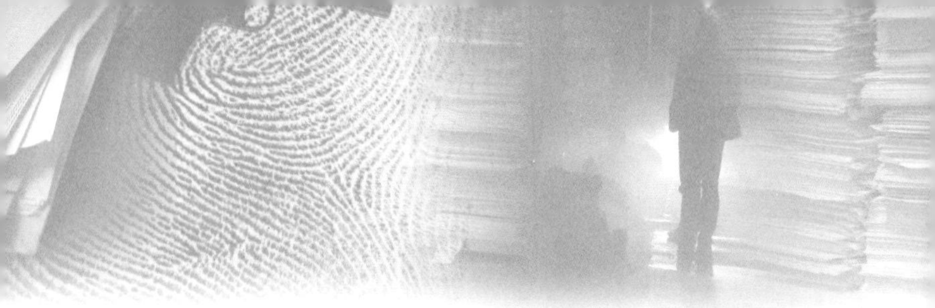

area and who was known to the police as a troublemaker. Joe and Thad walked to a deserted house a mile away, Thad still confused as to what was going on. It was only once they were there that Thad realized he had made a big mistake. Clark took him to a filthy upstairs room, laid him on the bed, and began to torture him by twisting his ankles until one of them broke. In extreme pain, Thad got up and struggled downstairs, but Clark followed him and pinned him down again, this time breaking his leg at the thigh. Clark then told Thad how much he liked to hear bones break, and continued to torture the boy for hours. In a sick parody of caring for the boy, Clark then fashioned crude bandages for his victim's legs from socks and braces, before leaving him alone. Clark went out of the house, thinking that Thad would never be able to escape now that his legs were broken.

A short while afterwards, Clark returned, this time with a girl, who sat with him in the living room and then left the house. Clark then discovered, to his surprise, that Thad had now dragged himself all the way to the kitchen, intending to escape. To punish him, Clark took him upstairs again and tortured him once more, this time threatening to kill him.

That evening, Clark went out again. Before he went, he made sure that his victim could not escape by locking him in a bedroom closet. Alone in the closet, Thad must have felt his time was running out, but he was determined not to give in to despair. He summoned all his willpower, and told himself that he would survive. He found an old electric guitar in the closet and managed to batter the door down with it. Somehow, he managed to drag himself downstairs again, and although he kept fainting with pain, was able to reach the telephone. He dialled 911 and told the operator where he was and what had happened.

Boasted about murder

The police came quickly to the house. There they found Thad with fractures to both of his legs, dehydrated and suffering enormous pain and fatigue. Thad told them the story of his ordeal, describing his tormentor, and saying that he had

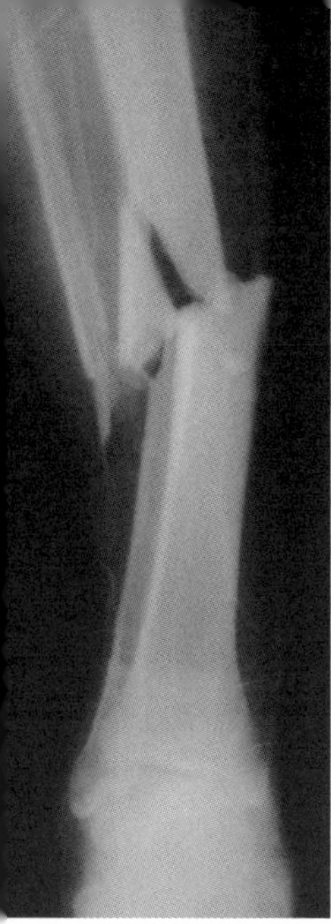

What was the draw of broken bones?

boasted about other victims he had injured, one of whom was Chris Steiner. The police immediately suspected local troublemaker Joe Clark. In Clark's bedroom, they found a chilling piece of evidence: a piece of paper with a list of boys' names on it. There were eighteen names under three separate headings: 'Get To Now'; 'Can Wait'; and 'The Leg Thing'. The names on the list all were local boys.

Clark was charged with attempted homicide, and was convicted. He was sentenced to a prison term of a hundred years. However, after this conviction, he chose to plead not guilty to the murder of Chris Steiner.

In order to find out what had happened to Steiner, his body had been exhumed. When it had been examined at the time of his death, it had not shown any signs of violent attack, and it had been unclear as to how he met his end. This time, with the knowledge of what had happened to Thad Phillips, Steiner's body was checked for bone breakages, and X-rays were taken. Sure enough, the X-rays revealed that his legs had been broken in four separate places, in the same way that Thad's were. It seemed that, having rendered Steiner's legs useless, the vicious Clark had then thrown the injured boy in the river, where he drowned.

Clark's parents tried to protect their son by claiming that he had been at home on the night of Steiner's murder, but it was known that Clark often surreptitiously left the house while his mother was sleeping. An inmate of the juvenile detention institution in which Clark had spent time also testified that Clark had boasted to him about killing a boy and afterwards draping his body over a tree in the river.

There was not much doubt that Clark was guilty as charged, and on 7 November 1997, Clark was convicted of the murder of Chris Steiner. He was sentenced to life imprisonment plus a further term of fifty years. To this day, Clark maintains that he was innocent of Steiner's murder, but – not surprisingly – there are few that believe him.

SCHUESSLER/ PETERSON: SLAUGHTER OF THE INNOCENTS

IN RECENT YEARS, COLD CASES HAVE BEEN SOLVED IN DIFFERENT WAYS. MOST OFTEN, IT HAS BEEN DNA PROFILING THAT HAS PROVIDED THE CONCRETE EVIDENCE NEEDED TO CONVICT SUSPECTED KILLERS, SOMETIMES DECADES AFTER THE EVENT.

In other cases, it has been dogged police work that, in the long run, has yielded results – tracking down the culprit through following up the slightest of leads, such as a name in a diary, or a watermark on an envelope. Then there are the cases where the perseverance of journalists, politicians, even friends and family, has pressurized the police and legal authorities to open the file and re-investigate the case once more.

But perhaps the most fascinating of all cold cases are the ones where witnesses have changed their minds and come forward to tell their story – people who saw or heard about a murder, but were unable or unwilling, for reasons of their own, to report it at the time; people whose consciences have continued to trouble them over the years, sometimes for decades.

In some cases, their relationship with the murderer may have changed so that they now feel free to speak: if they were once married to the murderer, they may

Collapsed in grief: Mrs Schuessler is carried into church to attend the double funeral of her murdered sons, John, 13, and Anton, 11

now be divorced; if the murderer was their lover or friend, there may have been a falling out. In others, witnesses may be pressurized by the police or the law courts to tell their story; this applies especially to prisoners, who are often offered lighter sentences or other privileges if they assist the police with their enquiries. And, of course, once the culprit is safely in police custody, witnesses usually feel less frightened to speak; indeed, once the threat of retribution has been removed, they are often keen to relieve themselves of the burden of their knowledge. For it remains a fact that most people, however corrupt or depraved, consider murder – especially, as in this case, the murder of innocent children – a crime that cannot be forgotten or forgiven.

Naked, bound bodies

In October 1955, the brutal killing of three young boys who were on their way home from a trip to the cinema shocked the citizens of Chicago. Today, it might be thought unwise to let three ten-year-olds travel to the cinema and back by

Fathers of the boys: Malcom Peterson (left) and Anton Schuessler at the inquest into the brutal slayings of their sons

themselves in the big, bustling city of Chicago, but at that time, the area on the north-west side of the city was more or less crime-free, and it was a common enough practice to let children walk the streets on their own during the daytime. Accordingly, John and Anton Schuessler and their friend Bobby Peterson set out from their homes with their parents' permission, to watch a matinee at the cinema in the Loop downtown. Unfortunately, they did not come straight back home after the show ended, but stayed around in town to enjoy themselves for a while.

At six o'clock that evening, they were seen in the lobby of the Garland Building at number 111, North Wabash. It was unclear why they were there. The only known link they had to the building was that Bobby Peterson had visited an eye doctor there, but that did not seem a reason for visiting the building on a Sunday.

The lobby was known at the time as a hang-out for gay men and prostitutes,

and it is possible that they may have been there to meet an older boy, John Wayne Gacy. Gacy, who later became one of America's most notorious killers of all time, was known to frequent the building at that period. He also lived not far from John and Anton's family home. However, there is no record that the boys met up, and the theory remains speculative. Whatever the reason they went to the lobby, they did not stay for very long, and continued on their way to a bowling alley on West Montrose called the Monte Cristo.

Witnesses later reported that a man of around fifty was seen hanging around the many young boys playing in the bowling alley and eating in the restaurant. It was unclear whether the three boys spoke to the man. After that, they hitched a ride at the intersection of Lawrence and Milwaukee Avenue. Again, this was not an uncommon practice at the time. However, by now the boys had spent the four dollars their parents had given them for the trip, and it was getting late. When they did not return by nine o'clock that night, their parents began to get worried about them, and contacted the police.

Beaten and strangled

The police conducted a search, but could not find the three boys. It was only when a salesman stopped to eat his lunch, two days later, that he saw the bodies of three children lying in a ditch not far from the river at Robinson Woods Indian Burial Grounds. The bodies were naked, bound up, and their eyes were covered with adhesive tape. There was evidence to show that they had been beaten and strangled. The coroner pronounced that their deaths had been caused through 'asphyxiation by suffocation', and a murder investigation was launched.

The crime deeply shocked the police officers, who described it as the worst murder scene they had ever witnessed. When news of the murders hit the headlines, the citizens of Chicago were horrified. As the father of one of the boys remarked, 'When you get to the point that children cannot go to the movies in the afternoon and get home safely, something is wrong with this country.'

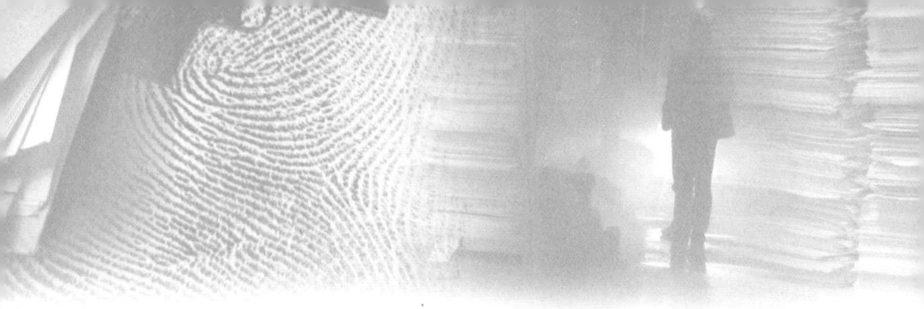

The case goes cold

The murder investigation began in Robinson Woods, with teams of officers searching the area to look for any clues such as items of clothing, footprints, or murder weapons. However, it appeared that the murderer had been very careful to cover up his traces. It was difficult to find fingerprints anywhere. Further examination of the bodies showed that they had probably been thrown from a car. Whoever had killed the boys had been an accomplished criminal, who was adept at escaping detection.

In retrospect it seems that, in the panic to find the killer, the police may have missed or misplaced vital clues. There were several different teams on the job, some of them from the central police department, and others from suburban forces. Perhaps for this reason, nothing of any significance was turned up; as it was, lack of co-ordination between the different teams, and the general prevailing air of confusion and shock, meant that little came out of the investigation – much to the disappointment of the officers concerned, and the public at large.

Out of respect for the three young victims, the Schuessler-Peterson case, as it became known, remained open. However, as the years went by, it became clear that no initiatives were being taken to move the investigation on. It was not until 1977, however, when the police were investigating the disappearance of candy heiress Helen Brach (described on page 56), that new and very promising information came to light – information that was to lead, through witnesses, to the boys' killer.

The murderer found

During the investigation, police talked to an informant named William Wemette who mentioned in passing that a man named Kenneth Hansen was known in some circles to have committed the murders. At the time of the murders, Hansen was twenty-two years old. He was working as a stable hand for a violent fraudster named Silas Jayne, who was notorious in the racing world as a cold-blooded

Justice is served: Kenneth Hansen on the day of his sentence in October 1995, a full 40 years after he beat and strangled three boys to death

killer. Jayne had actually been convicted of murdering his own brother, and had served a prison sentence for the crime.

Police investigators then talked to a number of other witnesses who, up to that time, had remained quiet about the stories involving Hansen and the three children. Apparently, Hansen had bragged to several men that he had lured the boys to his stables, telling them that he wanted to show them some special horses there. Once they were at the stables, he had sexually assaulted the boys, and had then strangled them. Shockingly, his employer Jayne had known of the killings, and had burned down the stables so as to destroy any clues. Not only that, but Jayne had actually collected insurance money on the buildings.

In August 1994, Hansen was arrested and charged with the murders. The following year, he was brought to trial. At the trial, the prosecution produced four witnesses who had been young men at the time of the murders. They were all now serving prison sentences in jail. The witnesses told how Hansen had promised them work in return for sex, and how he had threatened to kill them – as he had the three young boys – if they should ever speak of what he had done. For more than forty years, they had lived with the knowledge of the child murders, but now they were able to come forward and bear witness to what had happened.

Kenneth Hansen was convicted of the three murders in September 1995. The presiding judge sentenced him to a term of two to three hundred years – in effect, life imprisonment. It had taken decades to find the boys' killer, but eventually, through the testimony of the witnesses, he was finally put in the place where he belonged – behind bars.

CAROL SMITH: THE WOMAN IN THE BOX

THE 'WOMAN IN THE BOX' REFERS TO A CASE SO TRAUMATIC TO ITS VICTIM THAT THE MEDIA HAVE UNIVERSALLY PROTECTED HER ANONYMITY TO THIS VERY DAY, TWENTY YEARS AFTER HER CASE FINALLY CAME TO TRIAL. EVEN TODAY, SHE IS REFERRED TO SIMPLY AS 'CAROL SMITH' (OR SOMETIMES 'COLLEEN STAN').

Twenty-year-old Carol was living in Eugene, Oregon, when she left one May morning in 1977 to visit her friend in Westwood, California, to wish her a happy birthday. It was a four-hundred mile trip, but this was the 1970s, and Carol shared the free-wheeling spirit of her times. She walked on down to Interstate 5 to hitch a ride with someone kind enough to give her a lift – but tragically chose the wrong car.

After four days with no news of Carol, her friends back in Eugene rang her family, but they had not heard from her either. When they found out she had never arrived in Westwood, alarm bells started ring: Carol had always been the sort of person who kept in touch with those close to her, and now nobody knew where she was. Her friends in Eugene filed a missing persons report with the local police department.

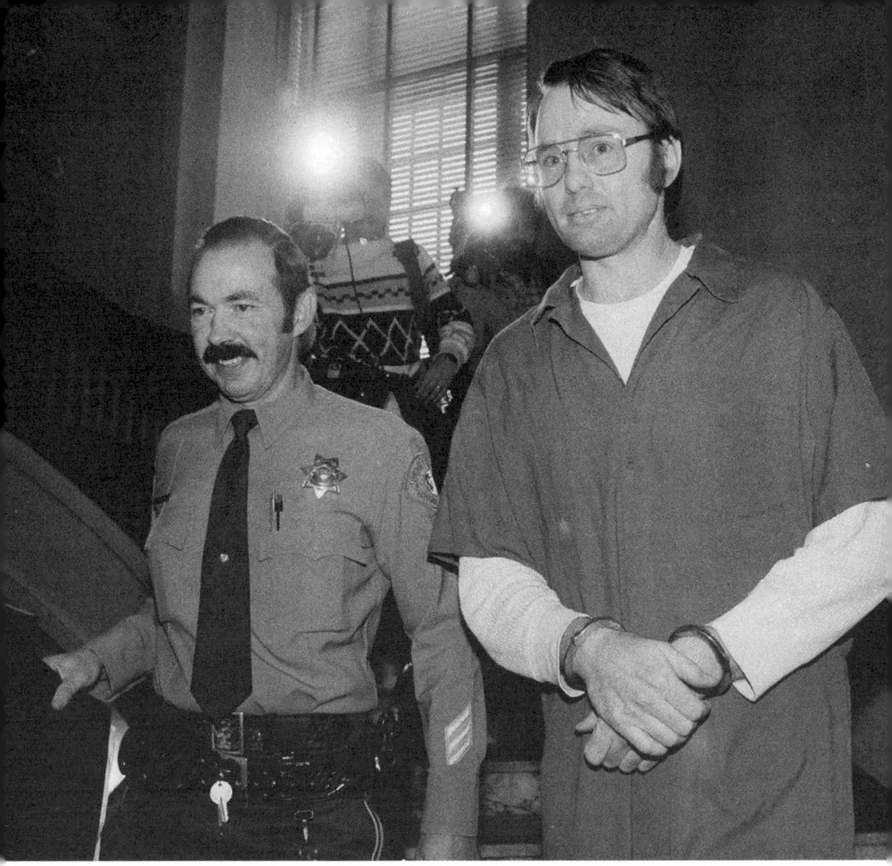

Looking surprisingly relaxed: Cameron Hooker, mid trial. Who knows how long he may have kept Carol locked up, if his wife had not turned him in

Miracle return

The first suspect was Carol's ex-husband (Carol had married when she was seventeen), but he was easily ruled out. Time passed, still with no sign of the young woman, and hope faded. Jenise, her sister, was the first to believe that she had been murdered, and as time went by, her case grew cold.

Then came an amazing development: more than two years after she disappeared, her sisters received a letter from her. It was full of affection, but short on detail: she had settled down somewhere with a man, 'Michael', and they were not to worry. She was sorry she could not be in touch more. Carol's family breathed a sigh of relief. Three years later, they finally got to see her again. She did not divulge much about her own life, but she was visibly overjoyed at seeing her family again. They were curious, of course, about what she had really been

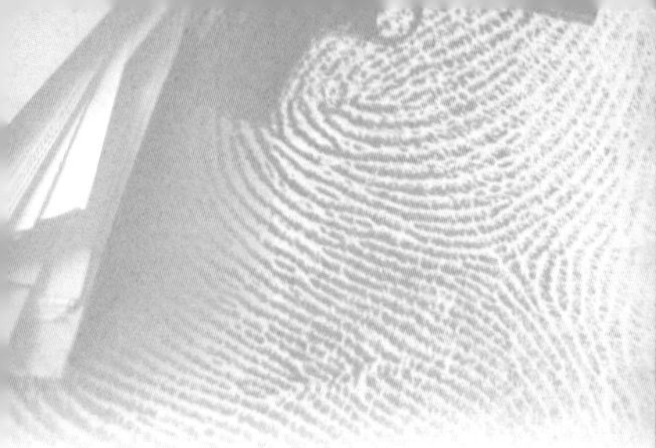

up to all that time, but they felt that they must have somehow offended her for her to go off like that, and they did not want to risk offending her again. They did not press her on her personal life but it might have been much better if they had, because Carol's life had turned into a living nightmare.

Cameron Hooker listens as he is sentenced to 104 years in prison

Head in a box

Carol had hitch-hiked all the way down to Red Bluff on the day she had left Eugene, back in 1977, and she only had another fifty miles to go when a blue Dodge Colt pulled over with a young family inside. She climbed in without hesitation, but however clean-cut the young couple and their baby appeared to be, she began to feel increasingly uncomfortable. The Hooker family seemed amiable enough, but deep down she felt something was wrong. When they stopped at a gas station she very nearly did not get back in the car, but when she did they were so nice to her she felt ashamed of herself. Then they made a detour to look at some ice caves. When they pulled off the road the man held a knife to her throat, and asked her if she was going to do whatever he said.

'Yes,' said Carol, desperately afraid. One word: yes. It destroyed her life, but it also saved it. She was then bound, blindfolded, and gagged. The man took a heavy soundproofed plywood box and fastened it to her head, which nearly suffocated her. Then she could feel them putting her into a sleeping bag.

Daily torture

When they got her back to their home she was kept in a large wooden box in the cellar, although Hooker would often take her out to torture her, or leave her dangling by her wrists from the ceiling. At other times she would be left in the box for days on end, with a bedpan. Initially she was fed a single meal every other day, but when her health began to seriously deteriorate Hooker and his wife began to feed her once a day. Hooker made her sign a contract which appeared to give their master-slave relationship some legally binding status. He told her she was registered with an entity called the Slave Company, who saw everything, and who would kill Carol's family if she ever ran away. Over the years, Carol's mind gave way and she came to believe it all.

After that, Carol's life got marginally easier. She was given handiwork to perform in a cage under the stairs. She was allowed out into the yard on weekends (neighbours believed she was a nanny). She was allowed to go jogging and to write home, albeit letters that were heavily censored. Janice Hooker took her out for a night's drinking, and Cameron Hooker escorted her for that single visit home, from whence she returned, for another three and a half years in captivity. Their hold on her was total.

The jealous wife

Jealousy was the key to Carol's freedom. Cameron had begun to have sex with Carol, and his wife was jealous. She confessed to her pastor, and he phoned the police. When the police came, she showed them the remains of an earlier victim who had not been as pliant as Carol, and who had been shot in the belly.

Janice Hooker plea bargained and was set free. Cameron Hooker was sentenced to life imprisonment. Even at the trial it was a close run thing, with the victim showing no signs of hostility towards her former captor of seven years. Some say it was only the physical scars of her torture that swung the jury, but whatever the truth, after so many years of horrifying cruelty, justice was finally done.

DOUTHIT

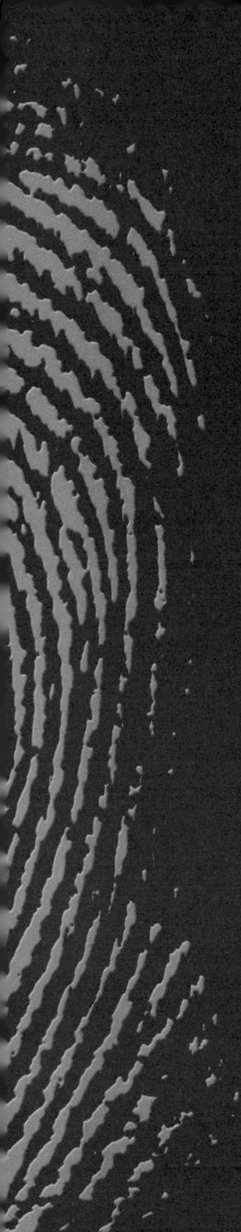

COLD COMFORT

In any of America's big cities, at any one time, there are hundreds of cold cases on police files. Of these, only a handful will ever be front-page news. There are many reasons why murders make the headlines: if the case involves a celebrity, it will almost certainly attract media attention – this was the situation with Jill Dando, a British TV personality who was murdered in cold-blood in an execution-style killing by a lonely obsessive who had been stalking her. The murder of a member of the wealthy elite, as in the case of candy heiress Helen Brach, also excites enormous interest: and Brach's case, with all its twists and turns in the cut-throat world of thoroughbred horseracing, is indeed a fascinating story. Then there are the high-profile political cases, such as that of Medgar Evers, the civil rights activist who was brutally murdered in 1963, but whose killer, white supremacist Byron de la Beckwith, was not brought to justice until 1994; or that of teenager Martha Moxley, whose killer's connections with the Kennedy family helped him evade justice for years, or so it was claimed. And finally, there are the cases, such as that of Hilda Murrell, an elderly lady living quietly in the British countryside, where a murder attracts attention because of a conspiracy theory that builds up around it – but which, in the end, proves to be less sinister than was supposed. What links all these cases is that they are the ones that hit the headlines, the murders that raise controversial issues in our society – whether to do with celebrity, wealth, class, politics or race.

02

GOODMAN, SCHWERNER AND CHANEY: THE FREEDOM RIDERS

EDGAR RAY KILLEN, KNOWN AS PREACHER KILLEN, WAS A MEMBER OF THE KU KLUX KLAN IN PHILADELPHIA, MISSISSIPPI, WHO IN 1964 ORGANIZED THE KILLING OF THREE CIVIL RIGHTS CAMPAIGNERS. AT THE TIME, KILLEN MANAGED TO GET AWAY WITH MURDER, BUT FORTY-ONE YEARS LATER HE WAS TO PAY THE PENALTY FOR THE CRIME HE HAD COMMITTED IN THE NAME OF WHITE SUPREMACY.

Terrible acts of violence

Killen was born in 1925, and grew up to become a sawmill operator. His other activities included working for the church as a part-time Baptist minister, and for the Ku Klux Klan as a klavern organizer, recruiting others to the cause. At this period, in the early 1960s, the Ku Klux Klan was a powerful force in Mississippi, encouraging a culture of extreme racism among ordinary white citizens. Terrible acts of violence against black people were committed on an almost daily basis in some areas; lynch mobs and firebombings of black churches were a common occurrence. These attacks very often went unpunished in the courts, since the influence of the Ku Klux Klan extended into the highest echelons of the judiciary, the police and the military.

By the 1960s, the situation in Mississippi had become the focus of a national

In 1952, racial segregation on inter-state buses was declared unconstitutional by the Supreme Court. Alabama in 1961 had still not embraced these changes, and a bus operating under non-segregation laws was firebombed. Fortunately, no-one was hurt

campaign among students at colleges across America. In what became known as the 'freedom summer' of 1964, dozens of young civil rights campaigners, both black and white, came down by bus, train, and plane from college campuses to the South, intending to challenge the 'Jim Crow' laws operating there. Among them were two young white men, Andrew Goodman and Michael Schwerner from New York, and a young black man, James Chaney from Mississippi.

At the start of their visit, the three friends set out to see the ruins of Mount Zion Church, a black church that had recently been firebombed. Unbeknown to them, their movements were being carefully tracked by Cecil Price, Deputy Sheriff of Neshoba County. On their return journey, the sheriff had the three men picked up for speeding, and held in the county jail.

Another bus load of 'freedom riders' – including four white college professors – arrives in Montgomery, Alabama in May 1961. Seating would have been mixed, rather than the division of white people at the front and black people at the back

Beaten and shot dead

Next, Sheriff Price contacted Killen, whom he knew to be the organizer of the Ku Klux Klan Neshoba Chapter, and told him that he was holding three civil rights campaigners in jail. He also said that he would be letting them out that evening. Killen then rounded up a large mob of bloodthirsty rednecks and told them of his plan to meet the campaigners on a country road as they left jail, and attack them. The mob, armed with rifles and other weapons, set out that evening, and caught

up with the three young college students as they walked down the deserted road. In a frenzied attack, they brutally beat the three friends and then shot them dead. Killen and his men later buried the bodies in an earthen dam.

Sheriff Price's plan had worked; yet ironically, the brutal murder of these young idealists, who wanted nothing more than peace and justice for all Americans, had the opposite effect of what the Southern racists intended. All over the country, people were so appalled at what had been allowed to happen in Mississippi that the civil rights campaign grew stronger than ever, and it was not long before a series of important civil rights laws were set in motion.

For many people, one of the most shocking aspects of the freedom riders' case was that, far from pursuing the perpetrators of the crime, the state of Mississippi initially allowed the murderers to go free. There appeared to be no attempt to arrest, charge and convict the culprits. Instead, the police and the judiciary closed ranks, blocking all attempts to have the killers brought to justice. In the end, the FBI, acting under the orders of President Lyndon Johnson, had to intervene to see that justice was done. Killen was arrested for the murders, along with eighteen others suspected of having joined the posse he had organized at Sheriff Price's request.

In 1967, the trial finally took place. By the end of it, most of the all-white jury

In the end, the FBI, acting under the orders of President Lyndon Johnson, had to intervene to see that justice was done.

were convinced that Killen was guilty and wanted to convict him. But there remained one member who felt unable, on principle, to convict a preacher. She held out against a decision to convict, so the jury was hung and could not reach a unanimous verdict. The prosecution decided against a retrial, even though it was clear that a conviction could probably have been gained next time, and once again Killen walked free. In an outcome that angered many civil rights campaigners, the men who had been found guilty of the murders received short prison sentences of no more than six years apiece.

Open racism

For the next forty-seven years, Killen continued to live in Mississippi, openly declaring his racist views. However, in 1999, an interview with Sam Bowers, a prominent leader of the Ku Klux Klan, was published, throwing new light on the case. In 2005, aged eighty, Killen was once more arrested for the murders.

Killen's trial was initially delayed because he had injured himself while chopping wood, breaking both of his legs. It finally took place in June 2005, and this time the jury were a mixed group of three black and nine white members. Killen attended court in a wheelchair, but this won him no sympathy, and he was duly convicted of manslaughter. The fact that he was not convicted of murder reflected his role as the organizer of the mob, rather than as the murderer himself.

The judge awarded Killen the maximum prison sentence he could: twenty years for each manslaughter, amounting to sixty years in total. It was obvious, of course, that Killen would die well before serving his term; however, the long sentence he received was a symbol of the authorities' commitment to civil rights, after years of neglecting their duty in this area.

It had taken decades for Killen to be brought to justice, but in the end, he was put behind bars. As eighty-three-year-old Carolyn Goodman, mother of Andrew Goodman, commented from her home in New York when she heard the news: 'I just knew that somehow this would happen – it's something that had to be.'

Killen's bond, which had allowed him to go free whilst appealing manslaughter convictions, was revoked in September 2005. He returned to jail

MARTHA MOXLEY: MURDER IN BELLE HAVEN

SOMETIMES MURDER INVESTIGATIONS LEAD NOWHERE. THE REASONS ARE MANY: FIRSTLY, A LACK OF LEADS, OF CLUES THAT COULD TELL THE POLICE SOMETHING ABOUT WHO MIGHT POSSIBLY HAVE COMMITTED THE CRIME. SECONDLY, INCOMPETENCE: LEADS THAT ARE NOT FOLLOWED UP, CLUES THAT ARE MISSED. THIRDLY AND PERHAPS MOST DISTURBING OF ALL, A LACK OF WILL: A FEAR OF TURNING UP EVIDENCE THAT COULD COMPROMISE THOSE IN HIGH PLACES.

In the case of Martha Moxley, a girl of fifteen who was brutally beaten to death in 1975, all these factors may have come into play. Whatever the truth of the matter, a few years after Martha's murder the case went completely cold. But over two decades later, the publication of a best-selling novel based on the murder reignited interest in the case. As a result, in 2002, twenty-seven years after Martha Moxley's brutal murder, the culprit was brought to trial, and convicted.

'Harmless pranks'

Martha Moxley was born in 1960 in San Francisco, California. Her family were prosperous, middle-class people who were able to offer their daughter all the privileges of a stable, well-to-do family life. In 1974, the family moved to the

A photo of Martha with her father, taken when she was thirteen. Her killer's guilt was protected by his family's wealth and status

neighbourhood of Belle Haven, a gated community in Greenwich, Connecticut. With its big houses and immaculately kept lawns, Belle Haven seemed the perfect place to raise a family. It was, above all, safe. But, as it turned out, the move was a fateful one: Greenwich proved to be anything but safe for Martha. A year after the family moved to Belle Haven, Martha Moxley was dead.

On the night of 30 October 1975, Martha set out with her friends to have some fun. The night before Halloween was known in the area as 'mischief night', when youngsters would amuse themselves by throwing eggs, spraying shaving cream, and trailing toilet paper around. These pranks were sometimes a nuisance, but usually harmless enough. However, that evening Martha and her girlfriends stopped at the house of the Skakel family to see their friends, brothers Tommy and Michael.

The Skakels were well known in the area. They were related to the Kennedy family through Ethel Kennedy, the wife of Robert F. Kennedy and were extremely wealthy. However, despite their social connections and money, there were serious problems in the family. The boys' mother, Anne Skakel, had died of cancer two years earlier, leaving her husband Rushton in charge of the household. After his wife's death, Rushton had taken to drinking excessively, and their teenage children had been allowed to run riot. They were a constant source of worry to the neighbours, and behaved in a rude, unruly, and undisciplined way. However, because of their class position, the bad behaviour of the young Skakels was largely tolerated – with dire consequences, as it turned out.

Beaten with a six-iron

Martha's mother became worried when her daughter did not return that night. She phoned Martha's father, who was out of town, as well as her neighbours and friends. Finally, she phoned the police, who although they drove around the area looking for her daughter, were unable to locate Martha. In the morning, the terrible truth was revealed. Martha's body was found under a tree not far from her house, beaten to death with a six-iron golf club. During the assault, the shaft had broken, and a piece of it had been used to stab her through the neck. Her jeans and underclothes had been pulled down, but she did not appear to have been sexually assaulted. When police took the golf club for analysis, they found that it was an expensive one, part of a set used by Anne Skakel.

There was other evidence that pointed to the Skakel boys. Martha's girlfriends reported seeing Tommy with Martha before they left for home that night. Looking for clues in Martha's diary, Martha's mother told police that her daughter had written about Tommy's sexual advances towards her, and how she had tried to repel them. Although the police searched the Skakel home, it was only a cursory visit. The police never issued a search warrant, which would have enabled them to do a proper search of the house without the owner's permission. Later, commentators criticized the police's conduct, claiming that Rushton Skakel's high-up connections and political influence had stopped them from going further.

Instead, the police followed up leads on other suspects, such as a tutor living with the Skakel family, a neighbour who lived close by the Moxleys; and several drifters who had been near the area on the night of the murder. However, these clues led nowhere, and by the 1980s, the investigation into Martha Moxley's murder had come to a grinding halt. In Belle Haven, it became an unmentionable subject: perhaps because of the Skakel influence, or perhaps because the wealthy inhabitants of this seemingly peaceful, well-tended residential area could not bear to remember that they were not, as they thought, safe from danger.

Teenage alcoholics

It was not until another Kennedy – William Kennedy Smith – became the centre of another drama that memories about Martha Moxley were jogged. In a high-profile case that attracted a great deal of media attention, Smith was accused of raping a woman in Palm Beach, Florida. He was acquitted, but rumours began

The head of the golf club prosecutors contended was used to kill Martha Moxley. It was part of a set owned by her killer's mother

to circulate that he knew something about the Moxley murder. In 1991 an article about the Moxley case, written by journalist Len Levitt, appeared in a local newspaper. Two years later, a novel by Dominick Dunne entitled *A Season in Purgatory* appeared, which was based on Martha's murder. The novel proved to be a best-seller. The author went on to meet Mark Fuhrman, whose notorious role in the O.J. Simpson case received enormous publicity. Fuhrman decided to look further into the Moxley case and, in 1998, published *Murder in Greenwich*. In it, he named Michael Skakel as the prime suspect.

Opinions as to why the murder had not been solved years before varied. Some felt that the wealth and influence of the Skakel family had prevented the investigation from going further, while others pointed to police inexperience as the cause. After all, Greenwich was not a place where murder happened very frequently – at the time of Martha's murder, there had not been a murder in the area for thirty years. However, all agreed that now, the case had to be given a boost, and accordingly, in May 1998, a request for a grand jury investigation was granted.

A fit of jealousy

Under this new initiative, over fifty witnesses were called in, some of them pupils and staff of a rehabilitation programme Michael Skakel had taken

Michael Skakel enters court in Norwalk, Connecticut. The Connecticut Supreme Court upheld his murder conviction of 2002. He is serving 20 years to life in prison

part in at Elan School in Maine. He had apparently confessed to Martha's murder during that time. Other witnesses, such as the tutor in the Skakel household at the time of the murder, talked about Michael's disturbed behaviour. He was reported, on one occasion, to have killed a squirrel when out golfing, and pinned it, crucifix-like, over a hole. By his own admission, he had been an alcoholic from his early teens, and had suffered abuse from his father. He had been devastated by his mother's death, and had felt that she was the only person holding together the dysfunctional Skakel family.

As it emerged, from an early age both Michael and his older brother, Tommy, had been extremely disturbed, difficult children. In all, there were seven Skakel children, and there were numerous family problems throughout their childhood. Rushton Skakel had left his children to their own devices, and the older ones among them regularly drank and smoked pot. On the night of Martha's murder, Tommy and Michael had been drinking heavily in front of their younger brothers and sisters, and their tutor Kenneth Littleton. Martha and her friends had visited, and she and Tommy had begun to make amorous advances towards each other.

What also transpired was that, after the murder, police initially investigated Tommy as a suspect. He took two lie detector tests, one of which he failed, and one of which he passed. However, after this, his father Rushton withdrew from the process, refusing to make Tommy available for further investigation. The fact that the police accepted this, and ceased their enquiry, had attracted criticism at the time. However, it later became clear that the police were following up the wrong suspect. It was Michael, not Tommy, who killed Martha, in a fit of jealousy because she appeared to prefer his older brother.

The results of the grand jury investigation were made public on 19 January 2000. Skakel was arrested on a charge of murder, and brought to trial two years later, on 4 May 2002. The jury took four days to reach a verdict, but when they did they found him guilty. He was sentenced to a term of life imprisonment.

HILDA MURRELL: COLD CONSPIRACY?

THE CASE OF HILDA MURRELL WAS ONE THAT FOR MANY MONTHS OCCUPIED THE BRITISH PRESS, BECAUSE OF THE VARIOUS POLITICAL CONSPIRACY THEORIES THAT AROSE AROUND IT. THE STORY READS LIKE AN AGATHA CHRISTIE THRILLER: MURRELL, A WOMAN IN HER SEVENTIES, LIVED QUIETLY IN THE COUNTRYSIDE, GROWING ROSES AND CAMPAIGNING AGAINST NUCLEAR ENERGY, UNTIL HER SUDDEN, VIOLENT DEATH IN 1984.

The local police took her murder to be the result of a botched robbery, but those in the political world thought that more sinister elements had been at work. Controversy raged, until the case was reviewed almost twenty years later. This time, with the help of DNA profiling, it was finally solved.

Stabbed and left to die

Hilda Murrell was born in 1906, and grew up in Shrewsbury, England. After attending Shrewsbury High School, she went on to study at Newnham College, Cambridge, and later became a renowned rose grower. She also became a conservationist, working to protect the wildlife of her native Shropshire. As part of her aim to protect the natural environment, she campaigned against nuclear energy, fundamentally disagreeing with the British government's strategy to

develop and expand its nuclear reactors.

In March 1984, Hilda Murrell's body was found dead in woodland near her home. There were several stab wounds on her body, but a post-mortem revealed that she had actually died from hypothermia. When local police visited her home, they found that an intruder had broken in. Their conclusion was that this was a robbery that had gone wrong. They thought that Murrell, aged seventy-eight, had put up a spirited fight and tried to stop the thief. It appeared that the thief had then forced her into her own car, driven her out to the woodlands, stabbed her, and left her to die.

A photograph of Hilda Murrell relaxing in the countryside – her murder was to spark conspiracy theories at high levels

British intelligence agents

However, after the murder, facts about Murrell's life emerged that made political activists and commentators suspicious. Shortly before her death, Murrell had been due to speak at an enquiry into the Sizewell reactor. Could the British government have been involved in the murder, to silence her and suppress crucial information? Not only this, but Murrell's nephew turned out to be a naval intelligence officer, Commander Robert Green, who had been involved in ordering the sinking of the *Belgrano*, an Argentinian ship, during the Falklands War in 1982. This had caused a major controversy in Britain at the time; many had opposed the war from the start, and the sinking of this ship, which caused the deaths of over three hundred sailors, caused enormous public protest – especially when it was claimed that the ship had been sailing away from the area of conflict. Could

British intelligence agents have been searching her house to obtain sensitive documents belonging to Mr Green about the sinking of the *Belgrano*, and ended up murdering her as a cover-up?

The main proponent of the latter theory was the Labour MP Tam Dalyell. He was backed by the Liberal MP Paddy Ashdown, who called for a public inquiry into the matter. In response, Murrell's nephew Robert Green, now retired, argued that his aunt's death had been nothing to do with the sinking of the *Belgrano*. He pointed out that his aunt had been a prominent opponent of nuclear power, and as such would probably have been listed by the government as a subversive. The implication was that if there were any secrets to come out, they would be more likely to emerge from this line of enquiry.

Freemasons and occultists

The police, however, continued to discount these theories, contending that Hilda Murrell had met her death as the result of a straightforward break-in by a vicious burglar. Dalyell countered this by saying that there were inconsistencies in the police records, and that there was evidence at the scene of the crime to show that the intrusion was not a simple break-in but the work of intelligence officers. For example, the phone line was cut in such a way that callers could ring in but

Dial 'M' for murder: the ripped telephone cord was at the centre of some of the many conspiracy theories surrounding the death of Hilda Murrell

not out. (The police denied this, however, saying that the phone had simply been pulled out of the wall.) Undeterred, Dalyell cited a confidential source which had led him to make the allegations.

Of course, the claim that Hilda Murrell had been brutally murdered by British intelligence officers, in the course of trying to suppress damaging evidence about the sinking of the *Belgrano*, electrified the media. If it could be proved, the Conservative government – now at a peak of popularity after winning the Falklands War – would be under serious threat. An avalanche of commentary followed, which included not only newspaper articles and parliamentary debates, but television documentaries, books, and even stage plays. More and more conspiracy theories arose: Murrell was a nuclear expert and was about to report terrible dangers at Sizewell; or that the investigation had been sabotaged by Freemasons in the police force; or even that occultists were to blame.

DNA evidence

None of this could be proved, however, and eventually interest in the case died away. It was not until twenty years later, in 2004, that the truth finally came to light. With advances in DNA profiling, the case was reopened and reviewed, and this time police were able to match up blood samples from the scene of the crime to those of a local labourer, Andrew George. George was charged with the kidnapping and murder of Hilda Murrell, and brought to trial. He was convicted and received a life sentence for the crime he had committed at the age of sixteen. After the trial, the police detective at the head of the investigation commented simply, 'I told you so'.

This, therefore, was a case that was allowed to go cold when, if everyone had accepted the obvious explanation in the first place, the culprit could have been brought to justice straight away. And had it not been for the fact that Murrell's murder was turned into a political issue, to suit the agenda of the warring factions of the time, it might have been solved many years earlier.

HELEN BRACH: THE MURDERED HEIRESS

THE CASE OF HELEN BRACH, THE HEIRESS WHO MYSTERIOUSLY DISAPPEARED IN 1975, IS ONE OF THE MOST SURPRISING IN UNITED STATES LEGAL HISTORY. WITH NO WITNESSES, NO BODY, AND NO LEADS FOR POLICE TO FOLLOW UP, THE INVESTIGATION WENT COLD SHORTLY AFTER HER DEATH – EVEN THOUGH, CLEARLY, SOMEONE HAD KILLED HER FOR HER MONEY.

Then, in a surprise twist, the case was warmed up many years later, and the man responsible for her murder finally brought to justice. Chillingly, however, it was the fact that the heiress left so much money sitting in the bank, rather than that she herself was missed, that had prompted a re-investigation of the case.

The hat-check girl and the millionaire

Helen Brach was born Helen Vorhees, and came from a working-class Midwestern family in Ohio. She lived most of her life in workaday circumstances, without much money and was working as a hat-check girl when she met her millionaire husband-to-be, Frank Brach. Frank was the son of Emil Brach, an immigrant who had come up with a new method for making caramel, and had founded a massively successful candy empire, E.J. Brach and Sons. His son

One of the last photographs taken of Helen Brach shows a rather lonely looking woman – just the type her killer preyed on

Frank proved an astute businessman, and subsequently had made millions for the company since then.

When Frank and Helen met, Frank was in the midst of a messy divorce. Not long after he divorced, he and Helen were married. The couple had no children – Helen was forty by the time she married, for the second time, and had no children by her first brief marriage. When Frank retired, the Brachs divided their time between their home in Chicago and a rented property in Palm Beach, Florida. Helen was generous with her new-found wealth, particularly with respect to her family, and bought her mother and brother new houses to live in. However, she did not flaunt her money or parade it in high society, as many other women in the same position would have done. In many ways, she remained a down-to-earth Midwesterner, who was careful not to spend too much on unnecessary fripperies.

Helen and Frank Brach lived comfortably, and uneventfully, for twenty years, until Frank died in 1970, at the age of seventy-nine. This left Helen with a fortune of twenty million dollars. Typically, she continued to live quietly, keeping in touch with her friends and family by phone, and caring for her pet animals. Her two dogs, named Candy and Sugar, became devoted companions, and she went to great lengths to make sure that they were properly looked after. In a rare show of extravagance, when the dogs died, she had them buried in an expensive pink marble grave. Her love of animals also led her to give money to charities, such as the Chicago Zoo.

The shady horse dealer

Although not interested in the glitzy parties of Chicago's rich elite, Helen did take an interest in racing, and after Frank died, expressed a wish to own some horses. She got to know Richard Bailey, the owner of a stables and country club. He was a charming, good-looking man but he had a reputation for shady dealing. He also had a reputation as a ladies' man of the worst kind: he would wine and dine rich old women, particularly widows, and extract money from them by asking them to buy his horses, most of which cost considerably less than he sold them for. He also often asked the women for a temporary loan which he never paid back. He stopped at nothing to gain their confidence: he would pretend to fall in love with them, have sex with them, even propose marriage, although he already had a wife. He made a specialty of choosing women who were ill, lonely, and even dying. There were more than a few elderly ladies who were smitten by his charms, so he made a good living, but those who knew how he operated despised him.

When Richard Bailey met Helen Brach, he must have thought he had hit pay dirt. Brach was considerably richer than any of his previous conquests, and obviously lonely. She enjoyed his company, and entrusted him with choosing her new racehorses for her. He began by selling her three horses, all of which were worth much less than she paid for them. However, with Brach, it seems, he bit off more than he could chew. She was not stupid, and despite the fact that she lived in a very private way, her fortune made her a powerful, well-known figure in Chicago society. Once she realized that Bailey was conning her, she threatened to expose his actions and report him to the police. Exactly what passed between them then, no one will ever know, but the outcome was that Bailey plotted to have her murdered.

The heiress vanishes

On 17 February 1977, Helen Brach went for a check-up at the Mayo Clinic, Rochester, Minnesota. This was the last time a reliable witness saw her alive.

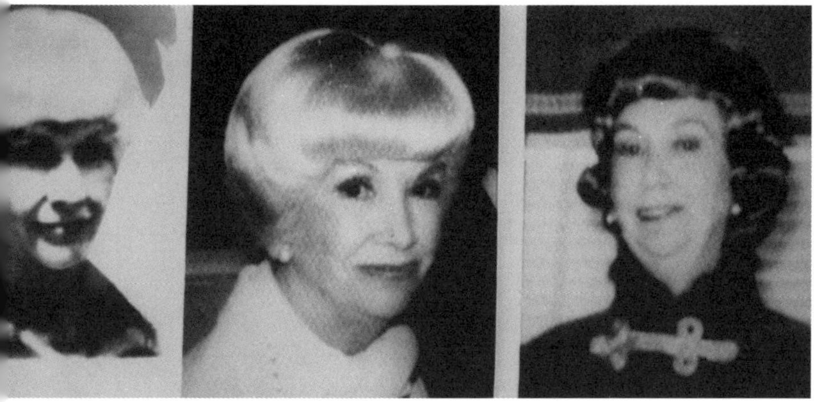

A more vivacious look: Helen Brach in her younger years was quiet, yet no push-over. When she realized what Richard Bailey was doing, she threatened to expose him. Instead, he had her killed

Then, according to her houseman, John Matlick, she flew to O'Hare Airport, where he picked her up. However, there is no record of her buying a plane ticket for the flight. For the next few days, while she prepared to go to Florida, no one heard from her, which was unusual for a woman who liked to chat daily to friends and family on the phone. Matlick then claims that he drove her to the airport for her flight to Florida, but that she did not have any luggage or a flight reservation, which again did not tally with the normal habits of this well-organized woman. Two weeks later, not having heard any more from her, Matlick reported her missing. So did another person – her brother, Charles Vorhees.

Suspicion immediately fell on Matlick and Vorhees, both of whom stood to gain from Brach's will. The pair admitted that they had destroyed her diary, which might have yielded valuable information about the days leading up to her disappearance, but said that she had asked them to do this should anything ever happen to her. Both their stories appeared questionable, but the police did not manage to find enough evidence to charge either of them, and dropped the case. Without a body, or any concrete information that could lead to finding out what had happened, the investigation began to dry up. Nobody seemed to care very much what had happened to Helen Brach, and her disappearance was soon forgotten. Yet her money – of course – was not, and it was the investigation into her accounts that finally brought the truth to light.

Everett Moore, Helen Brach's accountant, was a trustworthy man with an intimate knowledge of his client's day-to-day spending habits. He wanted to administrate Helen's estate, but the Continental Illinois Bank also felt it had a claim to this position. In the end, the court appointed an outside guardian, John Menk, to preside over the investigation. However, Menk did not get very far: Vorhees and Bailey both refused to talk, and since this was not a criminal investigation, there was no way that Menk could make them.

A lucky break

In 1984, almost ten years after her disappearance, Helen Brach was declared dead. Her estate was divided between the Helen Brach Foundation, Charles Vorhees and John Matlick. A meticulous accounting process began, presided over by Moore, and it was found that Matlick had embezzled thousands of dollars out of the estate after Brach had disappeared. In September 1993, Matlick was ordered to pay the estate back. Further investigations into the estate's accounts showed that Bailey had also defrauded Brach, and this time, once his name came up, the law did not let him go.

In 1989, an investigation had begun into the horse-racing business in Chicago, and in the process, Richard Bailey's name had come up. His frauds over selling the horses to Helen Brach soon became known to the investigators, and the case was taken up by Assistant US Attorney Steven Miller. His approach, he announced, was to 'follow the money and solve the murder'. By a lucky break, he and his team found a veterinarian, Dr Ross Hugi, who had had dealings with

Richard Bailey, helping him in his scams. Through Hugi, they found out about an infamous Chicago family, known as 'The Jayne Gang', who had been running organized crime in the horse business since the 1930s. Their leader was Silas Jayne, who was widely feared throughout the business as a man who would stop at nothing, including murder – he had even been responsible for the killing of his own brother. And one of Jayne's associates turned out to be none other than Helen Brach's erstwhile friend and horse dealer: Richard Bailey.

The right man brought to justice

This was an extraordinary twist to the Brach case that no one could have foreseen. Quite separately, Bailey's name had come up in another investigation. For the next five years, Miller and his team worked day and night to make the evidence against Bailey stick in the Brach case. Finally, in 1994, they were able to bring Bailey to court, charged with soliciting the murder of Helen Brach.

Initially, Bailey did not appear unduly troubled by the charge, since there was so little concrete evidence in the case against him. But gradually, as the list of elderly women whom he had defrauded was read out in court, his innocence appeared more and more questionable. Witnesses also took the stand to testify that he was a violent person, as well as a con man. Miller then built a case to show that Bailey had had a strong motive for killing Brach, because she – unlike all the others – had stood up to him and threatened to report his crimes to the police so that he would be put behind bars for the rest of his life.

And that, in the end, was exactly what happened. Bailey was convicted, and is currently serving his sentence in prison. Not only this, but in the process, a massive insurance fraud in the horse business was uncovered, and a string of crimes dating back to 1955, including homicide and arson, were solved. Thus it was that a case that went cold for almost twenty years finally resulted in the conviction of a notorious, cold-blooded killer and swindler who mistakenly thought that he could get away with murder.

FOUR YOUNG GIRLS: THE BIRMINGHAM CHURCH BOMBING

ON 15 SEPTEMBER 1963, ONE OF THE MOST SIGNIFICANT RACIALLY MOTIVATED TERRORIST ATTACKS EVER TO TAKE PLACE IN THE UNITED STATES OCCURRED AT THE 16TH STREET BAPTIST CHURCH, BIRMINGHAM, DURING A SERVICE. ON THAT QUIET SUNDAY MORNING, NINETEEN STICKS OF DYNAMITE, SECRETLY PLANTED BY KU KLUX KLAN MEMBERS IN THE CHURCH'S BASEMENT, DETONATED WITH A HUGE BLAST. FOUR TEENAGE GIRLS - DENISE MCNAIR, CAROLE ROBERTSON, ADDIE MAE COLLINS AND CYNTHIA WESLEY - WERE KILLED, AND TWENTY-TWO MORE OF THE CONGREGATION INJURED.

The bombing had been intended to intimidate the black people of Birmingham, who at the time were the subject of constant racist attacks, so much so that the city was becoming known as 'Bombingham'. But this proved to be one bomb too many. The people of Birmingham and America as a whole, both black and white, were outraged by this unprovoked assault on a peaceful group of citizens at prayer, and their calls for justice helped to foster the burgeoning civil rights movement of the day.

When the case came to trial, the police and legal authorities, under the aegis of Alabama's segregationist governor George Wallace, let the bombers off lightly, in true Southern style. However, resentment against the injustice of the incident continued to simmer, until many years later the case was reopened and the culprits finally brought to book.

Aftershock: Alabama State Troopers arrive in Birmingham to assist local officers at the scene of the church bombing which killed four girls and left twenty-two members of the congregation injured

The Birmingham church bombing eventually became one of the most renowned cold cases in United States legal history. As the mother of one of the victims, by that time aged eighty-two and in a wheelchair, commented more than three decades after the event: 'I'm very happy that justice finally came down today. I didn't know whether it would come in my lifetime.'

Rule of hate

In the mid 1960s, the Ku Klux Klan was continuing its rule of hate in the South. It was a secret society dedicated to the eradication and intimidation of black people, and its members had infiltrated the top echelons of the police and judiciary. Ordinary citizens were terrified of the Klan, who often took reprisals against white people as well as black, in response to what they saw as fraternizing with the enemy. In the city of Birmingham, which had a large black population, there were constant attacks on black leaders, and the perpetrators of these crimes were left unpunished, or given ludicrously lenient fines or prison sentences. By 1963, the situation had got completely out of hand.

Thousands gathered at a rally in New York to protest against the Birmingham church bombing. Some of those on the platform are James Baldwin, Medgar Evers, the Reverend Thomas Kilgore Jr, Bayard Rustin and Norman Thomas

On 15 September 1963, the congregation of the Bethel Baptist Church on 16th Street, Birmingham, assembled for Sunday worship. A group of eighty teenage girls went down to the basement with their teacher for a Sunday school class. At 10.22, the church exploded: walls collapsed, windows were blown out, and the air was filled with dust. Some survivors managed to crawl out of the rubble, but others could not move. When the rescue operation began, the mangled bodies of the four dead girls were recovered. The remnants of dynamite sticks were found under a flight of stairs leading to the basement.

A scene of carnage

The bombing provoked national outrage; even Governor Wallace condemned the crime. The FBI came under intense pressure to find the culprits and a reward was advertised for information leading to the men. Just fifteen days after the event, three men were arrested: Robert Chambliss, John Wesley Hall, and Charles Cagle. Known as a virulent racist and member of the Ku Klux Klan, 'Dynamite Bob' Chambliss had been observed on the day of the bombing standing stock-still watching the scene of carnage, while others around him rushed to help the victims. Chambliss was on friendly terms with the local police force, and was widely considered to have immunity from police prosecution as a result.

To the dismay of the nation, the racist Southern courts only gave the men six-month suspended jail sentences, and fined them a thousand dollars each. The Klan were jubilant. But public pressure continued to mount, and the FBI continued their investigations, concluding that the bombing was the work of four men, all members of the same Klan group. Their names were Robert Chambliss, Thomas Blanton Jnr, Bobby Frank Cherry and Herman Frank Cash.

FBI cover-up

The FBI assembled a mass of evidence against these men, but FBI boss J. Edgar Hoover suppressed the information, fearing that a prosecution would fan the flames of the civil rights movement. Hoover was obsessed with destroying the reputation of Martin Luther King, whom he regarded as a Communist agent, and knew that the truth about the Birmingham bombing would help the civil rights leader's case. However, there were others who were more concerned that justice should be done. In 1970, the new Attorney General of Alabama, William J. Baxley, was elected, and made it his business to get to the bottom of the case, which had shocked him deeply as he was growing up.

Baxley put a great deal of effort into investigating the case, but after a few years became convinced that the only way it would be solved would be to reopen the suppressed FBI files. He threatened the FBI with exposure for withholding the information, and in 1976, the bureau finally allowed him access to the files. The following year, Robert Chambliss was brought to trial, and his niece, Elizabeth Cobbs, testified against him, along with numerous others. Chambliss received a sentence of life imprisonment, and died in 1985, still swearing to the very end that he was innocent.

Baxley had made himself too unpopular to win an election as governor of the state. Once he was out of power, the case grew colder and colder. However, fifteen years later, in 1997 it was finally reopened. The FBI were continuing to block the investigation, but new evidence had apparently come to light – Herman Frank Cash, one of the original suspects, had died, but Thomas Blanton and Bobby Frank Cherry were tracked down – Cherry living in a beaten-up trailer in Texas. The pair were arrested for murder.

A protest by numbers: Dr Martin Luther King is followed by the Reverend Fred Shuttlesworth, left, and Ralph Abernathy as they attend funeral services for the four girls killed in the bombing

Dr Martin Luther King, dressed in black robes, conducts a solemn church service for the four young African American girls killed in the Birmingham church bombing

Murder boasts

Blanton's trial in 2001, over thirty years after the event, attracted national attention. The FBI had planted a bug in his apartment, and, on the tape, he was heard talking about bombing the church. He was found guilty of murder and sentenced to life imprisonment. The case against Cherry took longer to bring to court, because his lawyers alleged that he was mentally unfit to be tried. However, eventually, the trial took place in 2002. His ex-wife and granddaughter testified against him, and secret FBI tapes revealed that he constantly boasted to his friends about bombing the church. Like Blanton, he was convicted of murder and sentenced to life imprisonment. Cherry died in prison two years later.

Thus it was that the perpetrators of the Birmingham church bombing were finally brought to justice in one of the oldest, coldest cases in United States legal history. In his oration at the girls' funeral, Dr Martin Luther King had said: 'God has a way of wringing good out of evil'. Decades after their death – and King's assassination too – with the power of the Ku Klux Klan diminished in the South, many felt that his words had finally come true.

LINDA LEON AND ESTEBAN MARTINEZ: DOUBLE HOMICIDE

THE CASE OF LINDA LEON AND ESTEBAN MARTINEZ IS A SHOCKING ONE. IT WAS A DOUBLE HOMICIDE, IN WHICH THE COUPLE WERE TORTURED AND MURDERED IN FRONT OF THEIR YOUNG CHILDREN. THE AFTERMATH WAS NO LESS SHOCKING: LEON AND MARTINEZ MADE THEIR LIVING AS DRUG DEALERS, WHICH MEANT THAT FEW IN THEIR CIRCLE WERE WILLING TO COME FORWARD WITH INFORMATION. NOBODY SEEMED TO CARE VERY MUCH ABOUT THE FATE OF A COUPLE OF DRUG DEALERS, EVEN WHERE THEIR CHILDREN WERE INVOLVED.

It was not until a determined detective named Wendell Stradford picked up the case that the investigation began to move. He believed that, however the victims earned their money, the perpetrators of the crime needed to be brought to justice. Leon and Martinez had been brutally murdered in the most horrific way, and their young children callously left alone with their mutilated, bleeding bodies. By the time Stradford began work, the case had been on the files of the New York City Police Department for a long time, and had gone completely cold, but he was determined to catch up with the culprits.

Stabbed in the ear

It was in the run-up to Christmas of 1996 that a 911 operator received a call from a six-year-old boy telling her that someone had killed his mother and father. At first, he was too upset to give the address, but the operator was eventually able

Detective Wendell Stradford (left) noticed one particular name that kept cropping up in the cold case file; that of the person who was to become the chief suspect of the case

to wheedle it out of him, and police officers were immediately sent there. Once at the apartment, they found a scene that was as heartbreaking as it was appalling: the dead parents were lying on the floor, bound with duct tape, their bodies covered in blood, with the children trying to nestle in against them.

When the officers spoke to the children, little by little the story began to emerge: that their mother Linda Leon, twenty-three, and their father, Esteban Martinez, twenty-nine, had had a visit from four people, two men and two women. While the women had sat with the children, the men had taken their parents to another room, and repeatedly stabbed them before shooting them dead.

Just another statistic

Although this was a double homicide, and the evidence showed that the perpetrators had been sadistic killers, the case was allowed to go cold. The annual rate of homicides in New York City is high, especially among those involved in drug dealing. Leon and Martinez soon became just another statistic on the files of a crime-ridden city, despite the fact that murderers were still on the loose and out there somewhere, waiting to torture and kill the next drug dealers that crossed them.

It was not until 1998 that the case reached the Cold Case Squad at New York City's Police Department and some action began to be taken. Detectives found out that the Drug Enforcement Agency had been on the tail of Martinez, who was a cocaine dealer, and thought that he had probably been killed by members of a Colombian drug cartel. The investigation into this dragged on until Detective Wendell Stradford noticed that the name Robert Mitchell kept cropping up. He noticed that one of the children had referred to a 'Tio Rob', Uncle Rob, who often visited the house. Stradford tracked down Mitchell, and an associate named Tavon Blackmon. When Blackmon was picked up by police, he admitted that he knew Mitchell. According to his story, Mitchell had boasted to him that he had 'smoked' a guy and his wife in New York. He had gone round to their apartment with his girlfriend Keisha Washington, her twin brother Kevin, and Kevin's girlfriend Nisey. They had stolen a kilo and a half of cocaine and crack from Martinez, and had also made off with thousands of dollars, which Mitchell had used to buy himself an expensive new car.

In 2001, the detectives on the case managed to track down Keisha Washington, who by now had split up with Mitchell and was living in Baltimore. Under the guise of helping her to find Mitchell and gain child support from him, they interviewed her. She spoke of a terrible incident that had estranged her from her brother Kevin, 'Something I can never make up for', as she called it. Now a born-again Christian, Washington was attempting to make a new start in life, away from Mitchell and his influence.

Screams and gunshots

Washington gave detectives enough information to know that they were, at last, on the right track. They interviewed her again, and found out more. She told them how Mitchell had persuaded her to visit Esteban Martinez and his family, saying that Martinez was causing him to lose money. Her role was to look after the children while Mitchell discussed the matter with Martinez. They met up with

Kevin and Nisey, and all went over to the apartment, where she and Nisey sat on the bed in the children's bedroom watching television with them. The children constantly asked for their parents and cried when Robert and Kevin came in, roughly told them to shut up, and searched for money.

Then the real nightmare started, as the children began to hear their mother screaming. Kevin was stabbing her in the ear, trying to get her to say where the drugs and money were hidden. Next there were gunshots, and the children became frantic. The women held them down, covering their mouths, and waited until the men were ready to go. The four adults left, leaving the children running out of the room, screaming and crying, with their dead parents lying on the floor.

After this interview, the police let Keisha Washington go, but only after taking fingerprints from her. They later found that her fingerprints matched those lifted from a soda can at the scene of the crime. They also managed to identify the fourth suspect in the killing: 'Nisey' was Denise Henderson, a thirty-four-year-old woman from Baltimore.

An 'ugly knife'

The police now concentrated their efforts on tracking down Kevin Washington. When the police caught up with him, he tried to blame the murders on Robert Mitchell, claiming that Mitchell had only said they were going to rob the couple, take the drugs and the money, and then leave. However, according to him, when they got to the apartment, Robert pulled a gun on Esteban. Kevin then admitted that the women bound Linda and Esteban with duct tape, and that he had tried to cut Linda's neck with what he called 'a wood knife'. However, it had a serrated edge and would not cut. (As one of the children had described it, 'that bad man had a ugly knife'.) This, Washington seemed to feel, was some kind of defence for his behaviour. He then reported that Mitchell had shot both Esteban and Linda dead. After that, the four had set off back to Maryland, where Mitchell had disposed of the gun in an empty lot.

Shopping for Christmas

Police now had enough evidence to arrest Kevin Washington and charge him with second-degree murder and robbery. While he was awaiting trial, they went after Denise Henderson, who gave them more information. She described how they had all put gloves on as they went up the stairs to the Martinez apartment. This seemed to point quite clearly to the fact that the crime was premeditated. When they got inside the apartment, she and Keisha were told to wait in the bedroom with the children. The women rifled through Linda's belongings, trying to placate the children as they did so. There were sounds of screaming and gunshots from the next room, and then the men ran in and told them all to leave. When Henderson left, she saw a body on the floor, but just jumped over it on the way out.

The police arrested and charged Keisha Washington and Denise Henderson. Along with Kevin Washington, they now had three of the four murderers. But Mitchell proved harder to get hold of. In the end, the police had to conduct night-time raids on the house of his mother and his girlfriend in an effort to catch him, but he was not there on either occasion. In the end, it was only by pretending that they had come to protect Mitchell's family from violent drug runners that they managed to find out where he was, in an apartment on the other side of town. When they raided the apartment, they found Mitchell cowering under a bed wearing nothing but his underpants.

'Uncle' Robert

Mitchell was arrested, and when police interviewed him, he told a different story. He said that he had gone over to the Martinez apartment with the intention of getting back money that he felt was owed to him. Esteban had been living the high life at his expense, he explained, cutting drugs with other substances, which made it hard for Mitchell to sell them. He had only wanted to get what was owing to him from Martinez, whom he referred to as 'Tony'. Mitchell blamed Kevin for initiating the violence, and said that he had had nothing to do with it. By the time

he heard the gunshots, he was already outside the apartment. He claimed that he only found out about Linda and Esteban's death later, and was angry because he knew the children could identify him as 'Tio Rob'; they had never met any of the others before, so he was afraid he would be held responsible for the murders, which he swore he did not commit.

When the four cases came before the courts, the women plea bargained. In exchange for agreeing to testify at the trials of the men, they got six- to twelve-year sentences, which included the time they had already served (they had been held in police custody during this time).

At Kevin Washington's trial, his twin sister Keisha testified against him, and the Martinez children, now aged thirteen, twelve, and ten were brought back from the Dominican Republic to attend the proceedings. As the trial went on, it emerged that, on that fateful day, Esteban had been shot first, so as to frighten Linda into handing over money and drugs hidden in the apartment. But, even after she told the men, they still shot her.

Kevin Washington denied the charge against him, but the jury did not believe him, and on 26 March 2004, he was found guilty of second-degree murder and first-degree robbery. The judge sentenced him to seventy-five years in prison. He showed no remorse for the crimes, and continued to maintain his innocence.

Today, Robert Mitchell is currently awaiting trial. At his arraignment, he pleaded not guilty to murder. Mitchell blames Kevin Washington for the murders, just as Washington blamed him, but it seems unlikely that he will be believed. After all, the investigation only took off when the eldest of the Martinez children, then aged six, identified 'Tio Robert' as the man who had visited his parents and then proceeded to torture and kill them. And when the boy takes the stand again to testify, now no longer a six-year-old but a young teenager, he will no doubt remember more about that fateful day when his parents, Linda Leon and Esteban Martinez, were decorating the family's apartment for Christmas and Tio Robert came to call.

MEDGAR EVERS: THE RACE CASE

THE CASE OF MEDGAR EVERS IS ONE OF THE MOST EXTRAORDINARY IN AMERICAN LEGAL HISTORY. AFTER HIS MURDER IN 1963, IT TOOK ALMOST THREE DECADES FOR JUSTICE TO BE DONE: BUT EVENTUALLY, BY A STRANGE TWIST OF FATE, IT WAS DONE, AND HIS NAME IS NOW REMEMBERED WITH PRIDE AS ONE OF THE MAJOR PIONEERS OF AMERICA'S CIVIL RIGHTS MOVEMENT.

Political activism

Evers was born in Decatur, Mississippi on 2 July 1925. As a young man he served in the United States army during the Second World War, and went on to enrol in business studies at Alcorn State University in Lorman, Mississippi. He was a keen student, involved with many activities, including playing team sports, singing in the college choir, taking part in the debating society, and editing the college newspaper. In fact, he was so successful that he was listed in the 'Who's Who' of American colleges.

At college, Evers met his wife, Myrlie Beasley, and the pair married in December 1951. After receiving his degree, the newly wed couple moved to Mound Bayou, Mississippi. Evers was a bright, ambitious young man, who was determined to combat the racism of the Mississippi establishment so that he

Grief and defiance: mourners march and sing through Jackson, Mississippi, in a funeral procession for slain civil rights leader, Medgar Evers

could follow his career path and raise his family in peace in the place where he had grown up.

His first job after leaving college was as an insurance salesman, travelling round the South. On his travels, he saw for himself the abject poverty in which many black families lived, and was determined to do something about it. He became more active in politics, joining the National Association for the Advancement of Coloured People (NAACP) and helping to organize boycotts of gasoline stations that were refusing to allow black people to use the restroom facilities. He also helped to set up local chapters of the NAACP around the Mississippi delta.

In 1952, in recognition of his efforts, Evers was appointed the first full-time field secretary of the NAACP in Mississippi. His job was to collect and disseminate information about civil rights violations. He also organized non-violent protests against segregation, for which he was imprisoned. He was badly beaten several times, but he refused to be intimidated and carried on with his political activism.

Fresh fingerprints on the gun

In 1954, Evers applied to the University of Mississippi to study law. At that time the university was segregated, but Evers cited the ruling of the Supreme Court in the case of Brown v. Board of Education which ruled that segregation was unconstitutional. When his application was rejected, Evers campaigned for the desegregation of the university. In 1962, the campaign finally bore fruit when it

The face of African America's despair: Medgar Evers' son and widow attend his funeral in June 1968

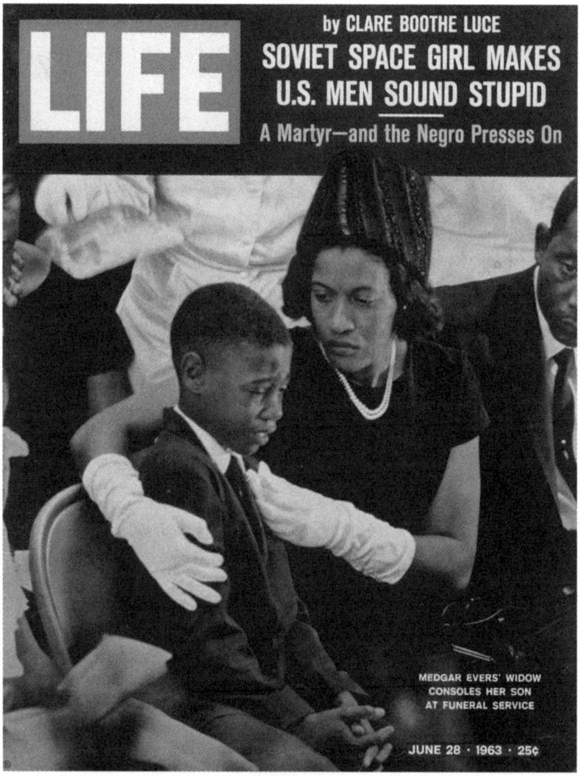

Medgar Evers (left), as the President of the Mississippi NAACP, was with James H Meredith – the first African American to go to the University of Mississippi – when Meredith announced he would be returning to the college, despite protest riots

enrolled its first black student, James Meredith. This triumph was at a cost, however: it sparked riots that left two people dead. In some quarters, Evers was blamed for inciting the violence, although he had always stated that 'violence is not the way' and had supported civil disobedience as a way of bringing about real change.

On 12 June 1963, Evers pulled into his driveway after a meeting and was brutally shot as he stepped out of his car, right outside his home. When the police were called, a gun was found in the bushes nearby, covered in fresh fingerprints. After analysis, there was no doubt who they belonged to: Byron de la Beckwith, a well-known figure in the local white segregationist movement. De la Beckwith had been heard to say that he wanted to kill Evers. After the murder, de la Beckwith was immediately arrested and charged, but despite the evidence, he was never convicted.

On two separate occasions, all-white juries failed to agree that de la Beckwith was guilty as charged. However, many years later, in 1989, new evidence came to light that the jury in both trials had been pressurized not to convict. There was also evidence of statements that de la Beckwith had made about the case, implying that he had committed the murder.

Body exhumed

In 1994, a new trial commenced, during which Evers' body had to be exhumed. It was found to be in a good enough state of preservation to corroborate the information. Byron de la Beckwith was finally convicted of the murder on 5 February 1994. He appealed against the verdict, but his appeal was rejected, and he went on to serve his sentence, dying in prison in 2001.

This was no ordinary cold case, however, in which new evidence alone resulted in a conviction. The years after Evers' death had seen a fundamental change in attitudes in the United States, as people began to realize the injustices of racism, prompted by the campaigns of the civil rights movement and the passing of a civil rights bill that enshrined the principles of equal rights in law. Over the years, it had become clear that segregation, and the violence involved in implementing it, was no longer excusable or acceptable in modern America.

As part of this process, the reputation of Medgar Evers grew. Immediately after his death, he was mourned nationally, and buried with honours at Arlington Cemetery. Nina Simone composed a song as a tribute to him (*Mississippi Goddamn*), as did Bob Dylan (*Only a Pawn in their Game*), which helped to establish him as a legendary figure. He became known as one of the earliest civil rights pioneers, whose courage and vision had been instrumental in kicking off

On two separate occasions, all-white juries failed to agree that de la Beckwith was guilty as charged.

The cold face of a killer: Byron de la Beckwith (right) is shown conferring with his attorney at Jackson police station after his arrest for the murder of civil rights leader, Medgar Evers

the civil rights movement in the United States. Thus, pressure to convict his murderer, and to overturn the biased decisions of the past trials, also grew. In a sense, the final Medgar Evers trial, decades after his death, was not just a trial of his murderer, but of the racist attitudes that had allowed his murder to take place, and to go unpunished for so many years.

JILL DANDO: CELEBRITY MURDER

THE MURDER OF JILL DANDO, THE POPULAR BRITISH TELEVISION PERSONALITY, SHOCKED THE NATION WHEN THE NEWS OF IT BROKE ON 26 APRIL 1999. THE PRE-MEDITATED KILLING OUTSIDE THE VICTIM'S HOUSE IN BROAD DAYLIGHT, WITH NO APPARENT MOTIVE OTHER THAN HATRED OF HER POPULARITY AND CELEBRITY, TERRIFIED MANY OF THOSE LIVING IN THE PUBLIC EYE. THE POLICE MOVED QUICKLY TO SOLVE THE MURDER – THE INVESTIGATION WAS ANNOUNCED BEFORE THE VICTIM WAS EVEN BURIED – AND AT FIRST IT SEEMED THAT THE KILLER WOULD SOON BE FOUND.

There were witnesses of a figure near the scene of the crime, and Ms Dando, like many other well-known figures, had received threatening letters and phone calls some time before her death. The police were determined to follow these leads up. However, as the months passed, it began to emerge these clues were leading nowhere; until finally, the case went completely cold. Almost a year after her death, the police were no closer to finding the culprit. The situation seemed hopeless, until police began to re-examine the evidence, and came up with something new.

Jill Dando was born on 9 November 1961, in Weston-super-Mare, a coastal town in the south-west of England. She studied journalism at university, and after a spell working on a local newspaper, went on to work for BBC radio and television. In 1986, she moved to London and began to work for the central

A huge outpouring of emotion: floral tributes outside the London home of the popular BBC TV presenter, Jill Dando, one week on from her murder

television network, becoming well known as a newsreader, and then as a host on several popular programmes, including the television show *Crimewatch*. The show featured cases that the police were working on, and asked members of the public to phone in with information to help solve crimes. Little did Dando or her colleagues know that her own murder would one day be featured on the show.

Shot in the head

By her late thirties, Dando's career was at its height. She had become a famous television personality, and was much in demand as a presenter, appearing in shows such as *Holiday*, in which she travelled to glamorous, exotic locations to report on the tourist attractions. Her private life was also happy: she had recently become engaged to gynaecologist Alan Farthing. Yet all this was to end tragically.

On the morning of 26 April 1999, Dando left her fiancé's house and went over to her own house in Fulham, West London. As she walked up to her front door, a stranger appeared and shot her at close range. A neighbour heard her screams and opened his window, to see a well-dressed man standing by her door. He then saw Dando lying bleeding on the ground, and hurried to help her. By the time he arrived at her door, the man had disappeared, and Dando was unconscious. She was taken to the nearest hospital, but it was too late. By the time she got there she had died, from a gunshot wound to the side of her head.

The reaction to her murder was one of horror – and incomprehension: there seemed no reason whatsoever why anyone would want to kill Dando. A murder investigation, known as Operation Oxborough, was immediately launched by the Metropolitan Police, London's police service. Three teams of detectives, headed by Chief Inspector Hamish Campbell, began the laborious process of interviewing the many people who had come into contact with Dando in the months leading up to her death, particularly those connected with the *Crimewatch* programme she had presented. It was thought that perhaps there might be some connection between her work there, which had sometimes brought her into contact with known criminals, and her death. *Crimewatch* itself featured the murder of their erstwhile presenter, asking for witnesses to the crime, which resulted in over five hundred people phoning in with information.

A number of witnesses...came forward, giving police some important clues as to who the killer might be.

Hit man or stalker?

There was also a meticulous forensic investigation of the scene of the crime. A gun cartridge was found, from a type of gun often used by drug dealers and professional criminals, a semi-automatic Browning pistol. This suggested that she had been killed by a hit man, or perhaps a stalker.

A number of witnesses who were near the scene of the crime on the morning in question came forward, giving police some important clues as to who the killer might be. A ten-year-old child being driven to school that day reported that he had seen a man dressed in old-fashioned clothes walking up and down the street. Another witness said that he had seen a man loitering in the street an hour before the killing, while others reported that a man had been seen running away shortly afterwards. There were also reports of a man talking on a mobile phone near a bus stop, out of breath and sweating. When a search of traffic monitoring videos was conducted, it showed a car speeding down a street near Dando's home.

Information was gathered from the witnesses and a composite of the chief suspect was drawn up. Unfortunately, the witness accounts, camera footage, composite sketch and psychological profile all failed to produce new leads in the investigation.

At first, the witness information and the video footage had seemed to offer many promising leads. The police took over a thousand statements, and

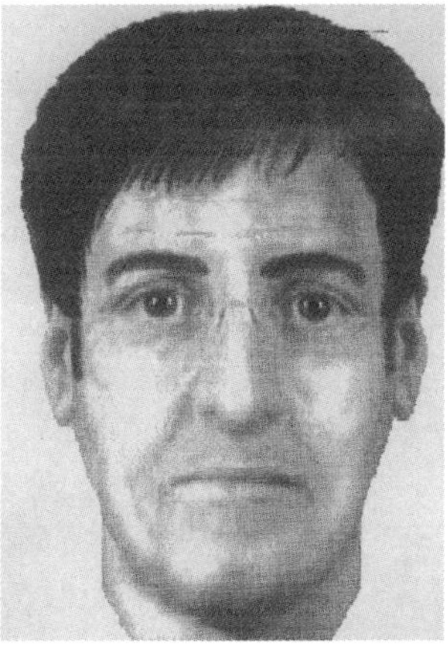

Despite a good likeness, the e-fit issued by Scotland Yard of the man police wanted to question in connection with the murder of Jill Dando failed to catch the killer for some time

talked to a total of more than two thousand five hundred people about the events. A composite drawing of the suspect was made, together with a psychological profile. But none of this led anywhere: three weeks after the murder, there were still no suspects, and no one was in custody.

The police thought they had got their man when they arrested 'loner' Barry George in May 2000

Public pressure to solve the case was intense, so Chief Inspector Campbell was replaced by Detective Chief Superintendent Brian Edwards, and a new team of detectives put on the case. A suspect was taken into police custody, only to be released shortly afterwards, uncharged.

The new team then came up with the theory, later shown to be false, that Dando was not murdered by a stalker. Some markings had been made on the bullet casing, suggesting that the killer had hammered it in such a way as to damp down the sound of the bullets firing. It was now thought that, because of the carefully planned, execution-style killing, Dando had been murdered by a cold-blooded professional, not a deranged loner. This change of tack, in retrospect, undoubtedly slowed the investigation down.

After three months, however, the police were still no nearer to finding Dando's killer. So the old theory, that she had been killed by a stalker, began to look likely once again. And it did seem that this was the more persuasive explanation: police looking into her personal affairs found that, on several occasions, a man had tried to gain access to private documents, and had tried to tamper with her telephone and electricity accounts. Yet this line of enquiry did not yield results either: a year after the murder, no one had been charged.

The obsessive loner

The police thought they had made the breakthrough when, after close surveillance, forty-year-old Barry Bulsara was arrested at his home on 25 May 2000. It emerged that Bulsara was not the suspect's real name, and that he had used several other false names as well. His actual name was Barry George.

The trial began on 4 May 2001. Barry George's history as a mentally unbalanced man obsessed with firearms, the BBC and with celebrity, came to light. After a brief stint as a messenger at the BBC, in 1977, he had continued reading the staff newspaper there. In 1982 he had joined a gun club, using the name Steve Majors, inspired by the Bionic Man television series. Police had found a picture of George in his flat, brandishing a handgun similar to the one used to shoot Dando in the head. They had also found pictures of thousands of women.

One of the major pieces of evidence offered by the prosecution was a particle of firearm residue found by forensic investigators in the pocket of a coat belonging to the accused. The main planks in George's defence were his mental disabilities, which, his counsel argued, would have made him incapable of committing such a crime; and witness reports to the effect that armed officers had been present at the time of George's arrest. The jury found George guilty by 10:1.

After the trial, George's previous crimes were made public. He had convictions for assaults against women, and once was found with a 21-inch hunting knife and a 50ft rope in the grounds of Kensington Palace, home of the Princess of Wales.

However, George's supporters were convinced of his innocence of the Dando murder, and after a lengthy campaign his case was referred to the Court of Appeal. Expert witnesses testified that gunshot residue was unreliable evidence; the particle could have come from another source. A re-trial was ordered.

When the new trial opened, in June 2008, the judge ruled the particle evidence inadmissible, thereby demolishing the prosecution's case, which then rested solely on witness identification. On 1 August 2008, George was acquitted, and a case the police thought they had solved remains open.

COLD-STEEL KILLERS

The random, repeat slayings of innocent victims, in a pattern that indicates an obsessive, mentally unbalanced mind, using methods that are often grotesque and ritualistic, is a horrifying and perplexing modern social phenomenon. These are the killers whose sheer, repetitive brutality and incomprehensible violence strike fear into today's urban citizens: those such as 'BTK', with his signature method of murder, 'Bind, Torture, Kill'; or The Green River Killer, whose total of forty-eight confessed murders makes him the most prolific serial killer in America.

These cases had police baffled for many years, and seemed unsolvable – until DNA profiling provided the crucial evidence needed to convict the killers. In this section, we look at the twists and turns of the cases over the years, and show how they finally came to be solved – along with others, such as that of British serial killers Fred and Rose West, a couple whose taste for torture, rape and murder, makes truly horrifying reading. Even more grotesque is the story of Albert Fish, whose taunting letters describing his demented activities finally led to his downfall.

We also look at less well-known killers such as John Robinson, who lured many of his victims through the internet; and Faryion Wardrip, the crazed 'minister' whose crimes also went undetected for many years. Finally, there are the stories of serial rapists: Gerald Parker, the so-called 'Bedroom Basher', and Dennis Rabbitt, aka the Southside Rapist, who were both caught through DNA profiling.

ALBERT FISH: MASOCHISTIC MULTIPLE MURDERER

ALBERT FISH HAS GONE DOWN IN HISTORY AS ONE OF THE MOST HORRIFYING SERIAL KILLERS EVER TO LIVE IN AMERICA. HE TORTURED AND MURDERED SEVERAL VICTIMS, INCLUDING CHILDREN, OVER A PERIOD OF TWENTY YEARS, AND ADMITTED TO HAVING MOLESTED HUNDREDS MORE. HE WAS A TERRIFYING, SADISTIC MURDERER, BUT WHAT WAS ALMOST AS DISTURBING WAS HIS EXTRAORDINARY PENCHANT FOR MASOCHISM: HE INFLICTED ALL KINDS OF BIZARRE TORTURES ON HIMSELF, AND WAS ALWAYS LOOKING FOR WOMEN AND CHILDREN TO ASSIST HIM IN THESE PERVERTED ACTIVITIES.

Yet despite his insane behaviour and his many crimes, police were unable to track him down, and for over five years, his trail went cold. Then, as a result of clever detective work on a letter Fish sent to the family of one of his victims, the chase was on again – and this time, the monster was caught.

Born Hamilton Fish in 1870, Albert was abandoned by his well-to-do family, who had a history of mental illness. He was sent to an orphanage in the Washington DC area, where he was often subjected to corporal punishment. He later claimed that he acquired a taste for being whipped and beaten as a result of this experience. In 1898 he married, and the couple went on to raise six children. Luckily for them, Fish did not take to beating them, but he did behave strangely, often asking his wife and children to spank him with a paddle which had nails stuck into it. His wife was also somewhat eccentric: she

Wisteria Cottage: Fish killed Grace Budd behind the house. He confessed to burying her bones there, which lead to a methodical search of the area surrounding the house by police

eventually ran off with another man, but then returned with her lover and hid him in the attic, until Fish found out and ordered the pair to leave. After that, Fish constantly looked through personal columns in newspapers: he was not interested in finding a new wife, but wanted a woman to beat him with the paddle. To this end, he wrote many obscene letters to widows and spinsters; but not surprisingly, he received no replies.

The grey-haired cannibal

Fish was an itinerant painter, drifting around the country in search of work. On his travels, he began to molest, abduct, torture, and murder children from the poor families that he encountered. He later claimed to have killed dozens of children in this way, committing a murder in every state of America. He said that he tied up his victims and whipped them with a belt studded with nails, to make their flesh tender for cooking. Then, having killed them, he ate them. He also ate their excrement, and drank their urine and blood. When he was finally caught, he confessed to killing a mentally retarded boy of ten in New York City in 1910; a young black boy in Washington in 1919; a four-year-old, William Gaffney, in 1929; and a five-year-old, Francis McDonnell, in Long Island in 1929. Amazingly, the families of these children – many of whom were at the lowest end of the social scale – found little redress from the law, so for many years Fish was able to continue his sickening activities without much opposition.

Grace Budd: Fish's ten-year-old victim was an attractive, confident little girl; a fact that probably led Fish to kill her

During this time, Fish exhibited characteristics of being completely insane, but again, nobody took much notice. His children reported that after their mother left, he would drag them to the family's summer home, Wisteria Cottage, and yell 'I am Christ' from a nearby hilltop. They also said that whenever there was a full moon, he would howl, and eat large quantities of raw meat. It later emerged that he was also engaged on a full-scale masochistic assault on his own body, poking needles into his genitals and pelvic area, and stuffing lighted balls of cotton wool into his rectum. In retrospect, it seems extraordinary that such a man was able to remain in charge of his children, all the while travelling the countryside freely; but according to many reliable witnesses, Fish had a mild, pleasant manner that made people trust him – or at least dismiss him as a harmless eccentric.

It was not until 1928, when Fish took a victim from a white, working-class New York family, that the authorities really began to take notice of him. At the age of fifty-eight – by this time with a string of child murders and molestations behind him – Fish responded to an advert from a young man wanting work, eighteen-year-old Edward Budd. Edward's father worked as a doorman, and Edward was seeking to improve the family finances by taking on a job. Fish visited the family

at their apartment and told them that his name was Frank Howard, a farmer from Long Island. He promised to hire Edward and pay him a good wage for work on the farm, saying that he would call back the following week. In the meantime, he sent the Budds a telegram, telling them the day he was to arrive.

Impressed with his good manners and his promise of well-paid work for their son, the Budds invited him to lunch. Fish behaved like an affectionate grandfather, handing out treats and dollar bills to the children. He then asked if he could take Edward's younger sister, ten-year-old Grace, to a children's party his married sister was holding at her house that evening. Tragically for all concerned, Grace's parents let her go. The pair left, Grace still wearing the white dress she had put on for church that morning. She was never seen again.

Murder hunt

The Budds were surprised when Mr Howard did not return with their daughter that evening, but presumed that the party had carried on late, and that they would return in the morning. When they did not return, Grace's father went to the address Mr Howard had given them, to look for his daughter. He found that there was no such address. He then went to the police station and reported his daughter missing. He was referred to the Missing Persons Bureau and, through this, came into contact with a veteran New York detective known for his tenacious police work: William King. King made enquiries, and soon found out that there was no Mr Howard and no farm on Long Island. King ordered the Western Union telegram service to look for the record of the telegram 'Howard' had sent the Budds – 'Howard' had asked for the Budds' copy back when he came to lunch, claiming that it had been wrongly addressed. King also tried to trace a carton of strawberries 'Howard' had given Mrs Budd, and found where he had purchased them. He gained a description of Fish, but from there, the clues petered out.

As it later emerged, Fish had taken Grace up to his summer house, Wisteria Cottage, where he had first of all let her run around, picking flowers. He had then tied her up, tortured, and killed her. He had eaten parts of the body and buried the rest near the house. Over a nine-day period, he had drunk her blood. Then he had gone on his way, continuing to travel the country in search of work, always on the look out to abduct children when the opportunity arose.

However, Fish had met his match with William King. King launched a massive manhunt, and soon the story hit the headlines. Grace's photograph appeared in many newspapers, and several witnesses came forward with new information. But even though all new leads were followed up, the police came no closer to finding Grace's murderer. There were several false alarms: in one instance, King was alerted to a man named Albert Corthell who was caught trying to abduct a girl from an adoption agency, but when he finally captured Corthell, it was found that he had been in jail at the time of Grace's murder. In another case, a man named Charles Pope was reported by his wife to have kidnapped young Grace. Pope was arrested and charged, but Mrs Budd pointed out that he was not the right man. It turned out that Pope's wife had accused him of the kidnapping out of spite, so he was released.

A new lead?

Meanwhile, there was another case in New York that could have led to finding the murderer, but did not. Albert Fish was arrested for sending obscene letters through the post. This time, Fish was posing as a Hollywood producer, offering to pay women to indulge his taste for sadomasochism. Fish was committed to a mental hospital, and stayed there for a month in 1930, during which time he behaved well. The psychiatrists acknowledged that he had sexual problems, but pronounced him harmless, and released him into the care of his daughter.

Four years later, despite his efforts, King was no nearer solving the case. However, on 11 November 1934, Mrs Budd received a horrible letter through the post, telling her the details of how the writer had cooked and eaten her daughter. Traumatized, Mrs Budd took the letter to King, who set about analyzing it for clues.

Grace Budd's bones lay buried for six years. Meticulous work by detective William King eventually led to Albert Fish, who had been apprehended on a number of occasions for other crimes but proclaimed 'harmless' and released

He noticed right away that the handwriting was the same as the original telegram from Western Union, and concluded that 'Mr Howard' and the letter-writer were one and the same. He then put the letter under a microscope and noticed a tiny set of letters on the back of the envelope; the initials of the New York Private

Chauffeur's Benevolent Association.

Detective King paid a visit to the association and began an exhaustive check on all the people who worked there, without much luck: there was no one who fitted the murderer's description. However, while he was there, one of the drivers paid him a visit to tell him that he might have left some of the association's stationery at a room he had used some time ago, in a cheap boarding house on 52nd Street, New York. King went there and spoke to the landlady, who told him that a man named Albert Fish, who fitted the murderer's description, had recently checked out, but that he still received a monthly check there from one of his sons. From time to time, Fish would drop by to pick up his mail.

Encouraged, King took a room in the boarding house, from where he could see the comings and goings of visitors. One day, while he was at work, he received a call from the landlady telling him that Fish was in the building. King rushed to the scene, and found the grey-haired old man quietly sipping tea with his landlady. He

Albert Fish in custody at the psychiatric unit of Grasslands Hospital, New York, where he had a further two needles extracted from his body, bringing the total to twenty-nine

asked Fish to come to the police station for questioning, whereupon Fish suddenly attacked him with a razor. Luckily, King was used to dealing with violent criminals, and soon had Fish handcuffed. He then found Fish's pockets full of knives and razors, and was sure that he had his man.

The case is solved

At the station, Fish began to confess his crimes, grinning insanely as he described Grace's murder in the most lurid detail. Detectives were sent to Wisteria Cottage and found that Fish was telling the truth: the remains of Grace's body were indeed buried near the house. And Grace was not Fish's only victim: Fish went on to describe other child murders he had committed since 1910. Police were doubly horrified to find that Fish had been arrested several times since Grace's murder, for relatively minor offences such as sending obscene material through the post, but that he had been set free every time.

A team of psychiatrists was then brought in to study Fish, who appeared to enjoy the experience, and boasted of his many perversions. Difficult as it was to believe him, he was telling the truth: when his pelvis was X-rayed, it was found to be full of needles. He was declared insane, but when he was brought to trial, the jury ignored this as a defence, and found him guilty of the murder of Grace Budd. The judge sentenced him to death by the electric chair. Fish went readily to his death, claiming that he was looking forward to being electrocuted, and that it would give him 'the supreme thrill of his life'. When he was brought to the chair, he even helped attendants strap him in to it.

A six-year manhunt for one of the most vicious killers of all time, Albert Fish – otherwise known as 'The Moon Maniac', 'The Gray Man', and 'The Brooklyn Vampire' – came to a satisfying end. Even though the case went cold for nearly six years, King never gave up hope: and, ultimately, his determination to bring the killer to justice, together with his meticulous attention to detail, paid off handsomely.

DENNIS LYNN RADER: BIND, TORTURE, KILL

BTK, WHICH STANDS FOR 'BIND, TORTURE AND KILL', WAS THE NAME BY WHICH DENNIS RADER, ONE OF AMERICA'S MOST NOTORIOUS SERIAL KILLERS, USED TO REFER TO HIMSELF. HIS CAREER OF CRIME SPANNED A PERIOD OF THIRTY YEARS, UNTIL THE CASE WAS FINALLY CRACKED OPEN.

At the beginning of his killing spree, Rader wrote letters to newspapers and to the police bragging about the murders, often describing macabre details of the crimes. Then the letters stopped, and after a long period of silence, resumed again. In this way, Rader taunted the authorities for years, terrorizing the public in the process. Today, many believe that, had forensic evidence and other clues been followed up more systematically, Rader could have been brought to justice many years earlier, and several of his victims spared their horrifying deaths.

Dennis Lynn Rader was born on 9 March 1945, the son of William and Dorothea Rader. The eldest of four brothers, he grew up in Wichita, Kansas, where he attended high school and college. As a young man, he joined the air force, and travelled abroad, returning home in 1970. A year later he married, and

Convicted serial killer Dennis Rader walks into the El Dorado Correctional Facility, Kansas. He admitted killing ten people in a thirty-year span, and was sentenced to ten consecutive life terms

the couple went on to have two children. During this time, he worked in a series of jobs, including a company that sold alarm systems for offices. He also studied at university, gaining a degree. He attended church regularly, becoming a church leader, and also became a Cub Scouts leader.

A mask found by Delores Davis' body in 1991. After Davis was dead, Rader tossed her under a bridge where the body decomposed

Hanging in the basement

His first known murder took place on 15 January 1974, when he broke into the home of the Otero family. The Otero parents' bodies, bound and gagged, were found by the couple's eldest son, Charlie, when he returned from school. When police searched the house, the bodies of his brother and sister were found: nine-year-old Joseph junior in a bedroom, his face covered by a hood, and eleven-year-old Josephine, partially undressed, hanging from a pipe in the basement. There were traces of semen at the scene of the crimes.

Nine months later, the local newspapers began to receive mystery calls. The killer directed reporters to a letter hidden in a book in the public library, in which he explained that he killed to satisfy a sexual perversion, referring to 'a monster' within him that he could not stop, and calling himself 'BTK': bind, torture, kill. The letter was badly written and spelt, but it was thought that that was just a ruse; many believed that the killer was actually quite well educated and intelligent.

Meanwhile, the murders continued. On 4 April 1974, Kathryn Bright and her brother Kevin were attacked in broad daylight by an intruder who was lying in wait at their home. Kevin was shot but managed to escape; his sister was stabbed in the abdomen and later died in hospital. Police did not, at the time, connect this killing with the BTK murders, even though there was evidence to show that the killer had tried to strangle Kathryn Bright.

The killer directed reporters to a letter hidden in a book in the public library, in which he explained that he killed to satisfy a sexual perversion.

Attention-seeking killer

The next killing did not come until three years later, when on 17 March 1977, Shirley Vian was found dead in her home, her neck bound with the same type of cord as the other BTK victims. As in the other incidents, the phone line was cut. Her three children thankfully escaped unharmed, although the killer locked them in the closet.

By this time, as the murders began to follow a pattern, the citizens of Wichita were beginning to panic. And sure enough, on 8 December 1977, there was another murder. This time, the killer alerted police to the scene of the crime, telling them the address where the murder had taken place. When police reached the scene, they found that, once again, the victim was a young woman, and once again she had been strangled, this time with a nylon stocking. However, this victim, Nancy Jo Fox, remained fully clothed.

Forensic evidence collected

For a while, the police heard no more news of BTK. Then more letters from him began to come in to the local papers. It seemed that the murderer was upset at the lack of attention he had received. He wanted the notoriety of Jack the Ripper or the Son of Sam, and he did not seem to be getting it.

Kathryn Bright and her brother Kevin were attacked...by an intruder who was lying in wait at their home. Kevin was shot but managed to escape; his sister was stabbed in the abdomen and later died...

Despite all his efforts to attract publicity, police were still unable to track down BTK. During the 1980s, a task force known informally as 'The Ghostbusters' was set up to sift through the evidence. Investigators found that all the killings had taken place within a three and a half mile radius and began to search the records of all white males within the area. The BTK letters were analysed, and the photocopying machine used to copy them was tracked down to the public library. The content of the letters was also studied, and leads followed up. DNA and semen samples were also taken for laboratory analysis. None of this led to the killer's arrest, however.

On 31 October 1987, another murder took place that many believed to be the work of BTK. The body of Shannon Olson, aged fifteen, was found partially naked in a wasteland area. She had been stabbed to death. Exactly two months later, Mary Fager returned to her home to find her husband Phillip shot dead and daughters Kelli and Sherri strangled in the basement. Soon afterwards, Mary received a letter from a person claiming to be BTK. Despite this evidence, the police arrested a builder who was doing some work on the house and charged him with the murders. The builder was later acquitted.

White-collared killer: it must have taken a cool head and some intelligence to have remained undetected – whilst committing such appalling crimes – for so long

Rader continued to paint a lurid picture of the murders, describing the 'hit kit' he took ...on his grisly missions: guns, ropes, handcuffs, and tape.

The 'hit kit'

Once again, the BTK case grew cold, and it was not until 2004 that another letter arrived, claiming responsibility for a murder committed in 1986. The letter contained the missing driving licence of a woman named Vicki Wegerle, who had been murdered at her home.

The following year the police finally made their arrest. They took Dennis Rader into custody, and he immediately confessed to the crimes, giving a detailed account of all of them. Two more crimes were added to the list, the killing of Marine Hedge in 1985, and Delores Davis in 1991. In court, Rader continued to paint a lurid picture of the murders, describing the 'hit kit' he took with him on his grisly missions: guns, ropes, handcuffs, and tape.

A trail of clues

To this day, no one knows what drove Rader to commit his hideous crimes, but what is clear is that over a period of three decades, he purposely left a trail of clues to taunt the police, clues that in retrospect could have led to his arrest many years earlier. For example, DNA analysis of Rader's semen matches that of the BTK semen left at the scene of several of the murders. Also, despite his college education, Rader was a poor writer and speller, and his mistakes matched up

Even the guilty deserve a fair trial: Rader's hand is shaken by his attorney after a hearing in El Dorado Correctional Facility. The judge recommended that he should receive treatment as a sexual offender whilst he serves the rest of his life in prison

exactly with those of the BTK letters. It also transpired that there were links between Rader and some of the victims: Joseph Otero had worked in the Air Force at the same time as Rader was there; Julie Otero and Kathryn Bright had worked for the same company as Rader. In addition, the payphones that BTK had used to report his crimes were, in some cases, very near his places of work; and the photocopiers he used could be traced to places where he had studied, including the university. Finally, there was the obvious clue that almost all his victims lived near his home; Marine Hedge even lived on the same street.

Eventually, of course, the net closed in, and Rader was arrested. But had forensic and other evidence been collected more systematically and the results analysed with more care, it seems that BTK could have been caught many years earlier, and the lives of several innocent victims spared.

CHESTER DEWAYNE TURNER: ANGEL OF DEATH

FOR SUCH A LARGE AND CRIME-RIDDEN CITY, LOS ANGELES HAS NOT PERHAPS SEEN QUITE AS MANY SERIAL KILLERS AS OTHER AMERICAN CITIES. FOR YEARS ITS MOST PROLIFIC SERIAL KILLERS WERE MICHAEL PLAYER, THE 'SKID ROW SLAYER', CONVICTED OF KILLING TEN TRANSIENTS IN THE DOWNTOWN AREA IN 1986, AND DOUGLAS CLARK, THE 'SUNSET STRIP KILLER', FOUND GUILTY OF HALF A DOZEN MURDERS IN 1980.

During the 1980s' crime wave, annual homicide figures sometimes topped a thousand a year. Perhaps this stark statistic acted as a smokescreen, which hindered police from apprehending, or even suspecting, that from 1987 onwards there was a killer at work who would eventually become one of the most prolific serial killers in the history of the city. All this changed when in 2001 the Los Angeles Police Department (LAPD) Cold Case Unit began looking at a single unsolved homicide, thanks in no small part to the use of a DNA record system and testing. In fact, the technology not only led officers to a prime suspect, it also freed an innocent man.

The Figueroa Street Strangler

Chester Dewayne Turner was not a native Californian, having been born in Warren, Arkansas, in 1968. When he was five his parents separated and his

Turner's mother worked hard to provide for her son, and he appeared to start off well in life. However, he then turned to crime, and never looked back

mother moved out west to live with her own father, taking her son with her. She worked hard to provide for him, holding down two jobs for much of his childhood. Turner was a pupil at 97th Street Elementary School and Gompers Middle School before dropping out of Locke High in his mid-teens. By this point he had grown to six foot two, and had a naturally heavy-set physique. His appearance was, by all accounts, intimidating and very noticeable.

After school, Turner went on to work for Domino's Pizza, where he began to carve out a promising career for himself, first as a delivery boy, then as a cook, and finally as a trainee manager. He then appears to have turned, quite suddenly, to a life of crime. From that point on, he spent the rest of his life in and out of jail, for a series of offences ranging from drug possession to theft. As time went on, Turner's life became more and more chaotic, as his drug use spiralled and his law-breaking became more frequent. He flitted from place to place, but always staying within the same small area, living in homeless shelters, at the

apartments of women friends and at his mother's house. When Turner's mother moved to Salt Lake City, Utah, in 1991, he went to live with her there on several occasions despite the fact that by this stage he was spending an increasing amount of time in prison.

After his first felony conviction for car theft in 1995, Turner returned to prison seven times, and these periods always coincided with a lull in murders taking place in and around the area where he lived. When he got out, they would start up again within a few weeks but at the time, however, nobody noticed.

In 2002, Turner was convicted of rape, the first violent crime on his record, and sentenced to eight years. After that, the killings stopped entirely. Again, nobody noticed, but it was this conviction that required him to give a DNA sample, and so began his journey on the long road to justice.

The killing years

Beginning in the late 1980s, a series of murders occurred in the same small area where Turner lived, within a couple of blocks either side of Figueroa Street, between Gage Avenue and 108th Street, a stretch itself of no more than a few dozen blocks. The thirteen murders began in 1987 and ended in 1998, most of them involving women who were involved in prostitution or were homeless, although some were just passers-by with the terrible luck to have been in the wrong place at the wrong time. The roll call of the dead is a long one.

In March 1987, the body of a twenty-one-year-old woman named Diane Johnson was spotted on the road by passing motorists. She was found strangled, and partially nude. In October that same year, Annette Ernest, twenty-six, met the same fate. Two years later, police received a call about a dead body in an alleyway. It turned out to be Anita Fishman, aged thirty-one. Again, she was found strangled and partially nude. In September the same year, the body of 27-year-old Regina Washington was discovered in the garage of an empty house. She was six months pregnant at the time. She had been asphyxiated.

In 1992 there were three murders in the area: Debra Williams, Mary Edwards, and Tammie Christmas, were found in September, November and December respectively. In early April the following year, the body of Andrea Tripplett, twenty-nine, was found by a builder. Only a month later, Desarae Jones, also twenty-nine, was killed. In 1995, there was Natalie Price, thirty-one; in 1996, Mildred Beasley, forty-five; and in 1997, Brenda Bries, thirty-seven. All were found strangled and in a state of undress.

The final victim was Paula Vance, forty-one, who was murdered in February 1998. It was this killing that put police on Turner's trail. It was recorded by no less than five different security cameras, each capturing various stages of the crime, but in each case, the camera panned away before the killer could be fully revealed; frustratingly, another second and the man's face would have come into view. As it was, all the police had to go on was a bulky silhouette.

CODIS and the Cold Case Unit

In 2001 LAPD detective Cliff Shephard became a member of the city's Cold Case Unit. He had over nine thousand unsolved homicides to choose from, but a specific brief to focus on those which were sexually motivated, and it was perhaps that tantalising silhouette that attracted him to the Vance murder. He had worked that part of town earlier in his career, and had always believed there were several serial killers in the area, although his hunch had never developed into a full-scale investigation.

Shephard's first step was to have the semen recovered from Vance's body sent to the laboratory for testing. The Serology Section of the LAPD's Scientific Investigation Division performed the extractions and made sure the resulting profiles were uploaded to the FBI-administered Combined DNA Identification System (CODIS) that is being compiled across the country. Then Shephard and his partner walked the streets again, as he had done before, as a beat cop, looking for registered sex offenders in the neighbourhood and handing out flyers.

...countless other homicides were fed into the computer... Soon, another match came back...and then another; and then another.

He spread the news that the Vance investigation was open again, in public and throughout the department, and made sure to consult other parts of the LAPD that might help him, like the Robbery-Homicide Division's special rape section. He even took the security camera footage to Paramount Studios where they enlarged it on a massive screen.

However, all this got him nowhere, at least initially. In deep frustration, he had almost decided to move on to another case when a call came back from the lab. The DNA from Vance matched that of a man already serving an eight-year sentence in California State Prison: Chester Dewayne Turner. As the suspect was already off the streets he posed no further immediate threat to the public, so Shephard was able to take the time to investigate the matter thoroughly. More samples from countless other homicides were fed into the computer, and CODIS crunched the numbers. Soon, another match came back (this one for Mildred Beasley); and then another; and then another.

'The number kept on growing,' Shephard said. 'We hit five, and thought, "Where are we going to end?"' All in all, this further testing took almost another year, as the detectives looked on in amazement. Eventually it peaked at thirteen. In October 2004, the police pressed charges against Turner.

Another victim?

Cliff Shephard had been with the LAPD for thirty years by the time he was investigating Turner. Unofficially, some colleagues might say this made him a bit set in his ways. Certainly, there were not many officers who would have checked Turner's DNA not just against unsolved murders but also against solved ones. Yet had he not, Dave Allen Jones would never have been exonerated of the murders of Debra Williams, Mary Edwards and Tammie Christmas.

Jones was a retarded part-time janitor with low IQ and a mental age of eight, who had incriminated himself while being interviewed (people like Jones frequently incriminate themselves under police questioning; the University of Chicago Law Review found that ninety-eight per cent of people with a low IQ or some form of mental disability believed they would be penalized in some way if they did not talk). His low IQ was further confirmed by the fact that when Jones signed his first letter for appeal, which was written for him by a fellow inmate, he misspelt his own first name.

However, thanks to DNA testing, it became clear that Jones was wrongly convicted of the murders. 'What's unusual here,' said Jones' lawyer, 'is that after he had his man and after he had found crimes that Mr Jones could not have done, he took that extra step. He suspended his own disbelief that such a mistake could happen and pursued it. And for that, Mr Jones and I have nothing but gratitude for him,' Gordon said.

Chester Dewayne Turner's trial for the series of murders will make him, if convicted, the most prolific serial killer ever to walk the streets of Los Angeles. He has pleaded not guilty to the killings. His defence lawyers are likely to focus on the possibility that the DNA samples might have been tampered with or carelessly maintained over the years. However, there are many who feel sure that the DNA evidence is incontrovertible, and that he will be convicted. If that happens, the relatives of the victims can be sure that the ghosts of their loved ones are finally laid to rest.

FRED AND ROSEMARY WEST: A KILLER COUPLE

FRED AND ROSEMARY WEST ARE AMONG THE MOST CHILLING SERIAL KILLERS OF ALL TIME. DURING THE 1970S, THEY MURDERED A STRING OF FEMALE VICTIMS, INCLUDING THEIR OWN DAUGHTER. YET DESPITE FREQUENT BRUSHES WITH THE POLICE, THE SEEMINGLY GOOD-NATURED BUILDER AND HIS WIFE WERE NEVER CONNECTED WITH THE MURDERS AT THE TIME THEY WERE COMMITTED.

In the decade that followed, police gave up the search for the girls who had gone missing in the area, and their files sat on the shelves collecting dust. The Wests would probably have got away with their crimes, had it not been for the fact that, in 1992, a young girl they had raped finally went to the police, and the whole story began – literally – to be unearthed.

Violence and sexual abuse

Fred and Rosemary West were both from deprived rural backgrounds, where violence and sexual abuse was not uncommon. Born in the village of Much Marcle in 1941, Fred was one of six children, and later claimed that incest was rife in the family. He was backward at school, and left at the age of fifteen scarcely able to read or write. At the age of seventeen he suffered a serious motorcycle accident that possibly caused damage to his brain: it was after this that his behaviour became increasingly out of control. He was eventually arrested for

The picture of a loving couple: not even their closest neighbours had any idea about what was going on behind the facade of a normal, busy family

having sex with an under-age girl, and narrowly avoided prison. His parents, finally tiring of his behaviour, threw him out of the family home.

Rosemary Letts, born in 1953 in Devon, was sexually abused from a young age by her schizophrenic father. Her mother suffered from severe depression. As a teenager, she was overweight and sexually precocious. When she met Fred, who was twelve years older than she, she idolized him, and soon became pregnant by him, even though she was not yet sixteen.

The murders begin

Fred had already been married, to prostitute Rena Costello, who had a mixed-race child called Charmaine from a previous relationship. Fred and Rena's own child, Anna Marie, was born shortly before the pair split up. Fred had then taken up with a friend of Rena's named Anna McFall, who was pregnant with Fred's child when, as later emerged, he murdered her, dismembering her body and burying it near the trailer where they lived. He was then free to concentrate on his relationship with his new girlfriend, Rosemary.

During this time, Fred was in and out of prison on minor charges such as non-payment of fines, while Rosemary was left in charge of the children – Charmaine, Anna Marie, and the couple's new daughter, Heather, born in 1970. Rosemary had a ferocious temper and was insanely cruel, especially to Charmaine. She abused the children while Fred was away, finally murdering Charmaine. Later, Fred buried the child's body under the house. Then, when Rena came looking for Charmaine, Fred murdered her too, burying her body in the countryside.

In 1972, the couple moved to a house in Cromwell Street, Gloucester, where Rosemary worked as a prostitute and continued to bear children, some of which were Fred's, and some of which were fathered by her clients. The basement of the house was used for deviant sexual activities, including the rape of their

Clearing work gets underway at Midland Road, Gloucester, a home of Fred West before he was married to Rosemary West

...when Rena came looking for Charmaine, Fred murdered her too, burying her body in the countryside.

daughter, Anna Marie, and a girl they employed to care for the children, Caroline Owens. When Owens went to the police, Fred West was tried for the rape, but – unbelievably – he was let off with a fine. Tragically, the next girl hired to care for the children, Lynda Gough, was not so lucky: she did not escape with her life, and was murdered and buried under the cellar. The couple went on to abduct, torture and murder more young women, in a killing spree that was as brutal as it was depraved: Carol Anne Cooper, Lucy Partington, Alison Chambers, Therese Siegenthaler, Shirley Hubbard, Juanita Mott, and Shirley Robinson all met their deaths in the most horrifying ways. The Wests even killed their own daughter, Heather, after she told friends about her bizarre home life. She was buried, like many of the other victims, in the garden of the house.

The case goes cold

Then, suddenly, the killings stopped. There have been many theories about why this came about: perhaps the Wests found other ways of satisfying their violent sexual impulses; or perhaps there were actually many other victims who were never missed, and whose deaths were never reported. The Wests were careful to choose their victims from the bottom of the social pile; often girls who had lost touch with their families, or who were working as prostitutes, whose relatives and friends would not come looking for them. (Lucy Partington, a middle-class university student and a relative of Martin Amis, was the exception.)

It looked as though the Wests had got away with their crimes, and that their victims would be forgotten. But in 1992, the couple's horrifying deeds came back to haunt them, when a young girl they had raped went to the police to report her ordeal. This time, her story was believed.

Buried under the patio

On 6 August 1992, police arrived at the house in Cromwell Street. They searched the house for pornography and found more than enough evidence to arrest the couple for rape and sodomy of a minor. One of West's perversions was to film his wife on video, engaging in sex with different partners, both men and women. The older West children, Stephen and Anna Marie, both made statements supporting the allegation of rape, but the case later collapsed when they withdrew these, under pressure from the family.

Meanwhile, the younger children had been taken away from their parents and placed in social care. Their carers began to notice that they often joked about their sister Heather being buried under the patio. This was reported to the police, who returned to the house in February 1994 and began to dig up the garden. To their horror, they not only found Heather's remains, but a total of nine other bodies in the garden. Later, other bodies under the cellar were dug up.

The troubled face of Heather West, who disappeared in 1987. Her remains were subsequently found, buried under the patio at 25, Cromwell Street

Fred West initially confessed to the murder of his daughter Heather, but then retracted the confession. It

seemed that he and Rosemary then made a pact, in which he would take the blame for the murder, emphasizing that his wife was not involved in any way. Accordingly, he re-confessed, stressing that Rosemary was not to blame, but by this time there was evidence to show that she too was responsible for the murder not only of Heather, but of many other victims as well.

Hanged in his cell

Fred West was charged with twelve murders in all, but before he could come to trial, he hanged himself in his prison cell, on New Year's Day in 1995. Rosemary maintained that she was innocent, but in October that same year, she was convicted of ten of the murders, and received a life sentence.

What would have happened if that young girl had not gone to the police to report her rape in 1992? Is it possible that Fred and Rosemary West would have continued to evade the law until the end of their natural lives, their crimes never discovered? What if the authorities had dismissed the girl's story, as they had dismissed that of Caroline Owens, the Wests' nanny, years before? It seems incredible that two people who had committed so many hideous murders could have gone undetected for so long – but that is what happened.

Perhaps it was a change in the social climate that helped to bring them to justice. Perhaps the permissive climate of the 1970s, in which the rules about sexual morality were beginning to be relaxed, impacted in a negative way on the underclass to which both Fred and Rosemary West belonged, so that the bizarre sexual behaviour that took place in their household went largely unnoticed and unremarked on by friends and neighbours, who might, in other times, have found it unacceptable.

However one explains it, the fact remains that it was only through the bravery of one young girl that the appalling brutality of this pair of vicious killers came to light, years after the murders happened, so that they finally received the punishment they deserved.

GARY LEON RIDGWAY: THE GREEN RIVER KILLER

THE TRIAL OF GARY LEON RIDGWAY, THE GREEN RIVER KILLER, WAS ONE OF THE MOST SENSATIONAL EVER TO TAKE PLACE IN AMERICA. RIDGWAY CONFESSED TO FORTY-EIGHT CONFIRMED MURDERS, WHICH MAKES HIM OFFICIALLY THE MOST PROLIFIC SERIAL KILLER IN AMERICAN HISTORY TO DATE. THE TOTAL COUNT OF HIS VICTIMS, WHO WERE MOSTLY PROSTITUTES, IS THOUGHT TO BE MUCH HIGHER. FOR MANY YEARS, HE ESCAPED DETECTION, EVEN THOUGH HE WAS CONSIDERED A SUSPECT.

A series of police task forces were mounted to solve the case, but time and time again, the trail went cold. In the end, it was DNA technology that finally enabled the police to nail this brutal killer, who is now serving a total of forty-eight life sentences in jail.

Teenage prostitutes

On 15 July 1982 a group of children discovered the body of sixteen-year-old Wendy Lee Coffield, in the Green River, Kent County, Washington State. She had drifted up against a piling near the Meeker Street Bridge, naked save for her tennis shoes, strangled by her own blue jeans. On 13 August that same year, a slaughterhouse worker came across the body of Deborah Bonner, and only two days after that, a man rafting the same stretch of river saw in the shallows what

Finger-tip search: investigators search for the remains of one of Gary Leon Ridgway's victims at an unknown location

turned out to be seventeen-year-old Cynthia Hinds. Next to her was another body, that of 31-year-old Marcia Chapman. All had been strangled. When police searched the area they found the body of another girl, Opal Mills, sixteen, on the nearby bank, dead by no more than twenty-four hours. The King County Sheriff's Department were hot on the heels of a serial killer, but it was as close as they would get for some time.

The victims of the Green River Killer belonged to a very specific demographic. All of them were women. All of them were believed to be prostitutes. And only a handful of them were older than twenty-one; almost half were eighteen or younger. Unfortunately, there was no shortage of these extremely vulnerable young women in the Washington area. Street prostitution in and around Seattle during the years of the Green River Killer was rife, and changes in state legislature had meant that young runaways could no longer be forcibly detained. As a result, there was an abundance of isolated, inexperienced and defenceless teenage girls who were prepared to climb into a car with a strange man as a way of making a living. When the act of running away had been decriminalized, police no longer even kept records on missing teenagers. Had they continued to do so, the monstrous scale of these murders might have been apparent much earlier.

Meanwhile the death toll had risen to sixteen. The killer was disposing of the bodies faster than the Sheriff's Department could discover them.

The killing ground

The area in which the prostitutes plied their trade straddled the city limits: when the Sheriff's Department were cracking down on the strip, these women went north to the city, and when the Seattle Police Department did the same, the women came back to the strip. The two forces never combined their efforts, and this problem in dealing with street prostitution made Seattle a rich killing ground for a serial killer.

Furthermore, vice officers for King County did not work weekends, when trade was busiest, and some even freelanced as security in local strip clubs, ensuring prostitutes were kept out of the lounges, forcing them out onto the streets, where they were most at risk. Similarly, in the city itself, police conducted a series of raids on brothels, although none of the girls that worked in them had ever fallen prey to the killer. When arrests were made in the red light district it was invariably the prostitute that was arrested, rather than her customer. There was no effort being made to keep a systematic record of these 'johns', not even of the licence plates on their cars. Inadvertently, the Green River Killer was being given a free hand.

On 16 August 1982, King County assembled its Green River Task Force. It was headed by Police Major Richard Kraske, and comprised twenty-five officers,

the biggest task force since the Ted Bundy murders seven years earlier – although, as it transpired, these officers were far less experienced. The day after Kraske's appointment, the task force staked out the river, and an overhead news helicopter broadcast their position to anyone with a television.

The first suspect emerged that September; a cab driver and ex-con named Melvin Wayne Foster, who had approached police to inform on other cabbies he considered suspicious. A psychological profile of the Green River Killer had already been performed by FBI agent John Douglas, and police considered Foster to fit perfectly. He was put under twenty-four-hour surveillance. After searches of his house, he was given a lie detector test, which he failed. Foster attributed his failure to a nervous condition. However, despite constant police observation, young women continued to disappear. Eventually, the task force had to admit they had been looking at the wrong man.

Meanwhile, the death toll had risen to sixteen. The killer was disposing of the bodies faster than the Sheriff's Department could discover them.

The first task force was disbanded when Sheriff Bernard Winckoski left his position in January 1983, to be replaced three months later by Sheriff Vern Thomas. Thomas began campaigning immediately for a new, larger task force. It took the rest of the year to organize, and to overcome his colleagues' concerns of the strain it would put on resources. By January 1984, a task force of forty officers was ready to look again at the Green River Killer, and every one of them must have felt the pressure: the killer was operating seemingly unhindered in a small area that was routinely patrolled by uniformed and plain clothes officers. Furthermore, while Sheriff Thomas had been planning and politicking, these murders had showed no sign of stopping.

Closing in on the killer

In a change of tactics, Thomas' task force began to arrest the prostitutes' clients instead of the prostitutes. Prior to this, arrests of women prostitutes were three

...he began visiting prostitutes for sex, and developed an intense hatred for these mostly young, inexperienced women.

times greater than the number of men arrested for trying to buy sex. Soon, the ratio was almost reversed, and the killings seemed to tail off. Progress was being made at last.

The killer had been scared away, or so it appeared. Police began to speculate that the culprit had moved, or was operating elsewhere. Although much good work had been done, the killer remained free, and morale in the task force began to plummet. Bodies continued to be discovered, but leads were few and far between. There were no physical descriptions of the killer, for the simple reason that no victim ever escaped.

When the sixth victim, Marie Malvar, got into a green pickup with a dark-haired man on 30 April 1983, her boyfriend was there to see it. He followed in his own car, noticing that the two seemed to be arguing, and then lost them at a traffic light near Des Moines. He reported her missing four days later. He returned to the area with her brother and father, and searched the streets, looking for the pickup, which they found in a driveway. The Des Moines police sent a detective, but she was not inside the house. It was three months before Des Moines police informed King County homicide of the incident. It was three years before King County factored it into their investigations (another victim, Kimi Kai Pitsor, had also been seen getting into a similar vehicle, but the two events were never connected).

Jose Malvar Jr, brother of Marie Malvar, on the witness stand at Gary Ridgway's trial. Malva Jr, his father and Marie's boyfriend searched the streets for the green pickup that Marie was last seen getting in to

A strange loner

Gary Ridgway was not unknown to police. He was a strange man that people described as friendly but odd, who had been raised in Seattle. His mother was a domineering woman, and he wet the bed as a child, but there was nothing in his childhood to suggest the burning rage that led him, as an adult, to become a serial killer. As a young man, he joined the Pentecostal church, and often collected for the church door to door. However, at the same period, he began visiting prostitutes for sex, and developed an intense hatred for these mostly young, inexperienced women. In 1980, he was accused of choking a prostitute, but police let him go. In 1982 he was interviewed in a car with prostitute Kelli McGinness (an eighteen-year-old who disappeared the following year), and the same year pleaded guilty to soliciting a decoy female police officer. In 1984, he

Ridgway confessed to killing forty-eight women over fifteen years. He was sentenced to life imprisonment — commuted from the death sentence in return for helping police find the bodies

approached Thomas' Green River Task Force to offer information, and was given a lie detector test, which he passed. Later that year, when police ascertained that he had contact with at least three of the victims, Ridgway finally became chief suspect. However, a house search provided no clues. In 1986, he passed another polygraph test ('I was too relaxed,' he later said). The following year, bodily samples were taken. Yet, despite the fact that he had been in the area, and had had contact with the women who were killed, Ridgway was not arrested.

The vital clue

After this period, the killings tailed off dramatically, and by 1991 the Green River Task Force was staffed by a single officer. But there were many who had not forgotten the victims of the Green River Killer, and who were determined to seek justice for their murders. In 2001 King County gained a new sheriff, Dave Reichert,

who formed a new team to solve the case, largely consisting of forensics and DNA experts. All viable evidence the county had collected was sent to the laboratory for investigation.

It was this initiative that was finally to yield results. The experts started with three of the earliest victims, killed in 1982 and 1983; Mills, Chapman, and Carol Christensen. Semen from the bodies was tested using new DNA technology and the match with Gary Ridgway's sample was positive. The Green River Killer had been found.

Justice at last

Ridgway was fifty-two years old when he was arrested on 30 November 2001 on four counts of murder. At first the killer maintained his innocence, but as testing continued on further remains, the evidence become incontrovertible. Two years later, he pleaded guilty to forty-eight counts of murder, mostly in 1982 and 1983, but one in 1990, and one as late as 1998.

In July 2003 Ridgway was moved from the county jail to an undisclosed location amid reports that he was prepared to co-operate if he could escape the death penalty. The plea bargain was defended by the prosecution as 'an avenue to the truth' for the victims and their families. While not all the families were happy with this, forty-one victims were named in court who would never otherwise have been mentioned, and as a result, some of the bodies were located and given proper burial.

It is generally thought that Gary Ridgway killed many more than forty-eight women. Chillingly, he himself has admitted he cannot remember all of the women he put to death. However, through a combination of police work and forensic technology, the case was finally solved, and he was made to pay for at least some of his hideous crimes. Today, with forty-eight life sentences to serve, there is absolutely no doubt that he will remain in jail for the rest of his life. After years of being hunted down, the Green River Killer is finally behind bars – for good.

DENNIS NATHANIEL RABBITT: THE SOUTHSIDE RAPIST

IT WAS YEARS BEFORE POLICE EVEN REALIZED WHAT WAS HAPPENING, BUT THEN RAPE IS PERHAPS THE MOST UNDER-REPORTED OF CRIMES. ACCORDING TO A 1996 SURVEY, ONLY THIRTY-NINE PER CENT OF SUCH CRIMES ARE EVER RELAYED TO LAW ENFORCEMENT OFFICIALS. EVEN SO, THERE ARE SOME WOMEN IN ST LOUIS, MISSOURI, WHO WOULD CLAIM BITTERLY THAT THE POLICE WOULD RATHER THE FIGURE WAS EVEN LESS.

Nevertheless, the following *modus operandi* of the person concerned began to emerge: between 1988 and 1997 an individual was breaking into women's houses at night, after they had gone to bed, usually through an unlocked door or open window. He wore a ski-mask and gloves to protect his identity. After the rape, he would usually force the victim to bathe, presumably to destroy any forensic evidence of his crime. The rapes took place in the better neighbourhoods of St Louis, towards the south of the city, areas that had always been relatively safe and crime-free, and for this anomaly the unknown criminal was dubbed the Southside Rapist. When DNA evidence finally brought his reign of terror to an end, the head of the city police department was compelled to open a new, dedicated crime lab, so no other criminal should escape this newer, longer arm of the law.

Under heavy police protection, including a bullet-proof vest and riot helmet, Dennis Rabbitt is transferred across state. So prolific was the range of his attacks, authorities in St Louis had to discuss which municipality would prosecute him first

The man behind the mask

Dennis Nathaniel Rabbitt was born in St Louis in 1957, to a middle-class family. His father was blind, and he was brought up mostly by his stepfather and his mother. During his adolescence, Rabbitt claims his mother drilled a hole in the bathroom door so she could watch him masturbate. Later in his teenage years he returned home one day to find his mother unconscious near the living room, and his stepfather upstairs in their bedroom, dead, with a gun in his hand and blood on the walls.

Rabbitt later said he knew something was wrong with him from an early age. By seventeen, his criminal record had begun, and he had become a known burglar. This did not stop him from leading the semblance of a normal life, however, and Rabbitt eventually married, and became the father of two. During this time he ran a bar and restaurant in downtown St Louis, and those that knew him described him as a typical married father. He was to describe the break-up of his marriage as one of the worst events in his life, although it was he who filed for divorce, in 1987. Observers who watched the case unfold were quick to point out that the first rape of which he was suspected occurred the following year.

The nightmare begins

As the police found out, while his *modus operandi* remained fairly consistent, there was no link between the victims of the Southside Rapist, other than that they were women, and they were vulnerable. He had no physical type, or racial preference. The age varied hugely too, starting in the mid-teens and ending in the early eighties. There were no other causative factors that linked them, none of the women knew each other, their daily movements were all different, and they worked and shopped in different areas. Yet each one would awake sometime in the night with a masked man sitting on their chest or legs, holding a knife at their throat, or pointing a gun at their head. Other than the rape itself he inflicted no other harm upon them, which would tend to categorize him as a power-assurance rapist, sometimes described by police as a 'gentleman rapist'. Rabbitt fits the profile reasonably well, being a man of average intelligence, who was rarely physically aggressive, who worried about his social status and may have been insecure about his masculinity, and who had failed at maintaining a strong romantic relationship. He also fantasized that the rape was consensual sex; desired and enjoyed by his female victim. It was anything but; even Jennifer Jewer, a woman of strong Baptist faith, who famously forgave him in court, eventually slid into a paralysing depression that cost her her job.

'To Serve And Protect'?

For over a decade, the St Louis Metropolitan Police were at a loss, while the rapes continued. 'He terrorized the city', Police Chief Joe Mokwa confessed. 'We didn't

know who he was or where he was going to strike next. We had no solid eyewitnesses to identify him.' In an attempt to narrow down the rapist's area of operations, they contacted James LeBeau, an administration of justice professor at the Southern Illinois University, in 1996. LeBeau was a pioneer of crime mapping (LeBeau: '[Crime mapping] is a generic term for taking locations of crimes and putting them on a map, putting spatial information in a geographical format'). But while crime mapping went on to prove itself useful for the purposes of trend-spotting and expending resources, it brought St Louis police no closer to the fleet-footed Southside Rapist.

Despite their best efforts, however, many remain critical of the Metropolitan Police's handling of the case, and their handling of rape cases in general. Statistically, St Louis officially had fewer rapes than most American cities, even while the Southside Rapist was at his busiest. As the *St Louis Post-Dispatch* has reported, this was largely because for decades huge numbers of rapes were never even filed on system, but simply kept as 'memos' for a period of months before being shredded. As late as 2005 the department had to increase its annual rape figure by fifty-three per cent. Physical evidence from rape kits was frequently destroyed too, often without ever having been analysed. In such a culture, critics argue, it is no wonder Dennis Rabbitt got away with so much for so long. There are also allegations that before Rabbitt was identified as the Southside Rapist he was found by police drunkenly passed out in public only a few houses away from where a rape had occurred the night before.

Manhunt

Frustrated, the police returned to their crime mapping. Could this new technique be honed and refined to produce a better result? The case had been cold for three years when they extended their search outside the Southside area and begun to look further afield, at rapes in less affluent parts of the city, even in other counties. With these extra cases taken into account, the profile of the perpetrator became clearer, and the list of suspects drastically shorter. Dennis Rabbitt, who had by now been arrested twice for attempted burglaries (failed rapes, he later confessed), was on the list. Crime mapping had worked after all: the officers had just needed to take in all of St Louis.

Under the guise of a peeping-tom investigation, they obtained a saliva sample from Rabbitt and analysed his DNA. It was a perfect match for the Southside Rapist, but when the tests were finished they found Rabbitt had left his new job in waste disposal and fled the city, almost immediately after giving the sample. The manhunt lasted for months. After an appearance on *America's Most Wanted*, a woman tipped off his whereabouts for a twenty-five thousand dollar reward. The FBI caught up with him in a motel in Albuquerque, New Mexico, with a fifteen-year-old girl in tow. He initially claimed to be Nathan Babbitt, but this modest alias could not hide his tattoos, which matched the description on record.

Behind bars

Dennis Rabbitt was tried not once but several times, in different counties, until he had been tried for each of the twenty rapes his DNA linked him to, and was found guilty on each count. He was sentenced to five life sentences in Missouri and an additional sixty years in Illinois. There are numerous but inconsistent reports that he has confessed to many more rapes than the twenty he was convicted of, from a total of twenty nine up to a hundred. 'It's only logical that there are many more rapes than we know about', St Louis Detective Mark Kennedy once said. 'Even if he averaged only four a year, that's more than one hundred rapes.'

In April 2005 Rabbitt was stabbed, repeatedly but not fatally, in the exercise grounds of the South Central Correctional Center, and moved elsewhere. Outside prison walls, St Louis police were so impressed by the efficacy of DNA evidence that they opened a new crime lab on Clarke Avenue that now oversees a hundred thousand cases a year. And in and around the Gateway City, a number of traumatized but relieved women are trying to get on with their lives.

JOHN EDWARD ROBINSON: THE ONLINE MURDERER

BETWEEN 1984 AND 1987 THREE WOMEN AND A BABY GIRL DISAPPEARED, ALL WITH CONNECTIONS TO DUBIOUS BUSINESSMAN JOHN ROBINSON, OF OVERLAND PARK, KANSAS. WHILE THE POLICE'S SUSPICIONS WERE AROUSED, EVIDENCE REMAINED THIN ON THE GROUND AND ROBINSON REMAINED FREE. THE FOUR FEMALES BECAME COLD CASES.

Thirteen years later the file on John Robinson was pulled out of the archives, when his penchant for brutal sex brought him to the attention of the police once more. This time the police put Robinson under covert surveillance, and discovered their man was a well-known figure in the shadowy world of bondage and domination. Soon there was enough evidence to secure a warrant for his arrest, and when police arrived at Robinson's home, the ugly truth about the missing women, and others, was revealed.

There were no signs of childhood trauma in Robinson's early years. In fact Robinson was a dedicated Eagle Scout, who went on to lead his own troop. His beginnings in Cicero, Illinois, gave no clue as to the monster he would become.

As he grew older, he dropped out of school, a Catholic prep seminary. Instead he attended a trades school in Kansas City, intending to become a radiologist. He began to fail his exams, but, in 1965 he had got a job as an X-ray technician, and papered the walls of his office with fake diplomas. They fooled no one, and he was eventually dismissed. He immediately started applying for other radiology jobs and it was not long before he ended up in another lab with another set of fake credentials. Robinson was becoming a pathological liar.

Soon after Robinson started his second job, the mask seemed to slip. He began embezzling and started a series of affairs and flings with patients and staff, sometimes under the pretence that his wife was dying and unable to have sex (he had got married when he was twenty-one, to a woman named Nancy Lynch). Eventually deputies led him away from the practice in handcuffs in 1969.

From conning to killing

At that point, Robinson's shaky hold on normality and decency finally gave up, and he became a career con-artist. He projected himself as a businessman philanthropist, and once even managed to give himself 'Man of The Year Award' at a mayoral dinner, although the local press exposed him, to the embarrassment and ridicule of his family. But Robinson was past caring: by the early 1990s he had been convicted of fraud four times. It was during this decades-long period of court supervision that Robinson contrived to kill eight women.

Perhaps his worst scam was the one he pulled on his own brother and sister-in-law. Don and Helen Robinson, unable to conceive, were hoping to adopt a child, and had put their names down at the end of some very long waiting lists. When John heard about it, of course, he had a much better idea: why not let him handle it? In 1983 he defrauded them of twenty-five thousand dollars for legal expenses and kept them on tenterhooks for two years, always promising them something was round the corner.

After that, it appears, he began to approach homes and charities for single mothers in a new guise, that of a wealthy philanthropist. Without verifiable references they ignored him. He decided he would have to find these vulnerable females on his own. He was able to collect nineteen-year-old Lisa Stasi and her baby daughter Tiffany from Lisa's sister-in-law's house by telling her he was taking her to a special housing project. Lisa Stasi was never seen again. Shortly afterwards he presented his brother with the baby and told Don that her mother had committed suicide in a shelter.

The next victim was Paula Godfrey, a teenager from Olathe, Kansas. Robinson 'owned' a string of companies that were little more than pieces of paper; Robinson said he could offer her a job in one of them, and taking him at his word, the young woman accepted. When she left her home in 1984, she explained to her parents that she was being sent away for training, and that she might be out of touch for a while. But as the weeks turned into months her family grew worried and approached police. Soon after filing a missing persons report, the Overland Park Police Department received a typed letter with Paula's signature at the bottom, explaining that she was healthy and happy, but did not want to see her family again. That was the last anybody heard of her. To this day, her remains have not been found.

John Robinson (right): in the dock for his crimes, at last

The typed letter was to become something of a motif in these disappearances. They were used after the murder of Lisa Stasi, and again with Catherine Clampitt, twenty-seven, who also disappeared after moving to Overland Park to work in one of Robinson's fake business in 1987. In 1993, Beverley Bonner, a prison librarian who Robinson had managed to seduce while in prison divorced her husband and moved to Kansas City, ostensibly to work for John Robinson. She was last seen alive in January 1994, although after a few more typed letters her killer was still able to collect her monthly alimony from a mail box in Olathe. In the following months Robinson would lure widow Sheila Faith, forty-five, and her fifteen-year-old wheelchair-bound daughter Debbie, from their home in Puebla, Colorado to Kansas. The two disappeared shortly after arriving, but Robinson would continue to collect Debbie's disability benefit until the day he was arrested.

Next, there was the 21-year-old Polish immigrant Izabela Lewicka, of West Lafayette, Indiana. Although she may have initially believed Robinson's claims about helping her career, he had by this time developed a penchant for master-slave sexual relationships, and Izabela was happy to indulge him in this. She signed a contract detailing the manner of her subjugation. She kept him amused for two years before Robinson grew bored and murdered her. He then turned to Suzette Trouten, a nurse's aide who also indulged in alternative sexual practices. They had met on the internet, on various bondage/sadomasochist sites Robinson visited, where he was known as 'The Slavemaster'. He offered her sixty thousand dollars to come down and look after his ailing father.

The ones that got away

Police had had their suspicions about John Robinson for a long time. His name was cropping up far too often on missing persons' reports. But in each case he had been careful to plant a story that would explain their disappearance, even arranging to have typed letters sent from other states and countries. In the absence of any dead bodies, they had to let the matter lie. For the families of the

victims, this case had definitely gone cold. But in 2000 the police realized they had the opportunity to press their investigation further.

They were helped significantly by Lore Remington, a friend of Suzette Trouten whom Robinson moved in on after murdering the Canadian nurse. Lore, worried about her friend's disappearance, decided to indulge him from a distance. Suzette's mother had already filed a report with the police, who were ready to tap into any phone calls between the pair. They asked Lore to continue her relationship with him so as to help their investigation, and she did so, playing him for the sake of her missing friend. The police began to covertly monitor Robinson's activities, and were shocked to discover the extent of his depravity. On the other side of thin walls in cheap motels, officers would have to listen to violent and abusive but apparently consensual sex. The surveillance lasted for two months, as Robinson's psychosis worsened and he grew more dangerous. Eventually, two women pressed charges for assault. The authorities used their evidence to secure a warrant to arrest Robinson and search his property.

Endgame

When police visited the killer at his family home they came straight out and confronted him with the full range of their suspicions, naming names that went back over twenty years. For once the silver-tongued fraudster fell silent. All that was needed was a thorough search of all of Robinson's property. In a remote, run-down ranch they found two sealed barrels containing the remains of Izabela Lewicka and Suzette Trouten. In a storage facility in Raymore, Missouri, they found two chemical drums holding the bodies of Beverly Bonner and Sheila Faith and her daughter. The other victims' remains were never found. Robinson confessed to the murder of these other missing women in a Missouri court in 2003 in a plea bargain to avoid the death penalty there. However, over the state line in Kansas, there was enough evidence for the prosecution to secure the death penalty at a second trial.

400 250 125 60 30

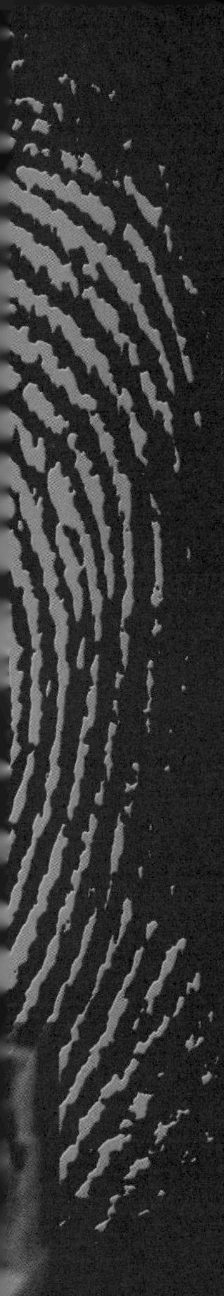

COOL HEADS

Police rely on many methods to detect crime. As well as DNA profiling – the single most important technological advance in the solving of cold cases (described in the next chapter) – there are other approaches which have yielded useful results. Here, we look at some of them, including the work of Frank Bender, forensic sculptor. Bender's first assignment was to build a bust of murderer John List for the TV programme, *America's Most Wanted.* List was a mass murderer who had slain his whole family before going into hiding for many years. Through a combination of psychological profiling, sound detective work, and sheer intuition, Bender was able to create a contemporary likeness of him that eventually led to his capture.

The 'Body Farm', brainchild of Dr William Bass, is the nickname of the Anthropology Research Facility at the University of Tennessee, Knoxville. Here, a team of scientists observe the decomposition of human corpses, in particular analysing insect activity. In this way, the team are able to help police determine, from the condition of a murder victim's corpse, exactly when the victim died, as well as other information. We also report on the work of Necrosearch, a dedicated team of specialists, from archeologists to biologists, whose methodical searching for 'clandestine gravesites' has helped police to solve crimes committed many years ago.

04

JERRY MCLENDON: A FORENSIC ANGLE WITH 'THE BODY FARM'

COLD CASES INVOLVING HOMICIDE CAN BE SOLVED IN A NUMBER OF SURPRISING WAYS. ONE OF THE MOST UNUSUAL IN THE HISTORY OF POLICE INVESTIGATIONS IS THE CASE OF JERRY MCLENDON. HE WENT MISSING ONE DAY, AND MIGHT NEVER HAVE BEEN DISCOVERED HAD IT NOT BEEN FOR THE TERRIBLE SMELL OF HIS ROTTING BODY.

It all began one afternoon in 1992, when some men who had set out to go hunting in the countryside passed a furniture dump. Coming from it was the most terrible smell, so pungent that the men decided to report the matter to the police. Detective Ronnie Minter from Henry County went to investigate the situation, and found a couch in the pile of furniture, where the smell appeared to be coming from. Underneath the couch he was horrified to find a human head. The rest of the man's body was wrapped in a sheet, and it had begun to rot down. Because of the dreadful state of the body, it was impossible to identify the victim, so a skin sample from the corpse's hand was taken and sent to the laboratory to gain a fingerprint. The sample was actually what is known as the epidermal glove, that is, the top layer of skin that covers the entire hand.

In order to make the fingerprint, the technician had to put the epidermal glove over his own hand, and then press down with his thumb to form a fingerprint.

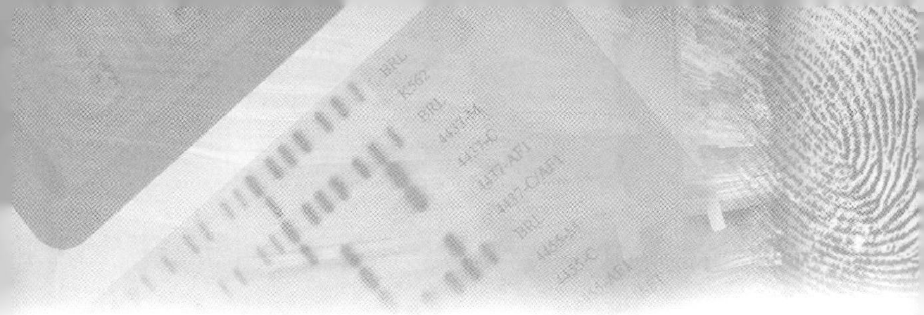

Unique: finger – and hand – print indentification is one of the oldest forms of forensic evidence, and is still as viable as DNA testing

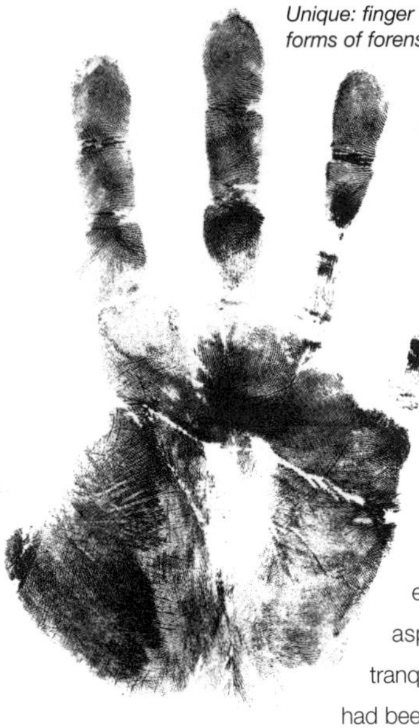

When the fingerprint was fed into the police's Automated Fingerprint Identification System, a match immediately came up. The victim turned out to be a man named Jerry McLendon, a 35-year-old sailor from Virginia Beach, Virginia. The next step was to find out who killed him – and why.

Drugged and suffocated

The badly decomposed body was taken for an autopsy. The pathologist who performed the task of examining it found that the victim had been killed by asphyxiation. There were also high levels of a tranquillizer in the victim's system, which indicated that he had been drugged before being suffocated.

Next, detectives found out where McLendon had lived and visited his apartment, hoping to find more clues as to what had happened. There, they found signs that the victim had fought his attacker, and noticed that in the bedroom there was a pillowcase stained with bodily fluids. They also noticed that the design of the pillowcase was the same as that of the sheet wrapped round the corpse's body.

When they looked through McLendon's accounts, they discovered that there had been withdrawals on it from a cash machine over the last few days, which was well after McLendon had died. They then followed up security cameras at the cashpoints, which showed a man and a woman withdrawing money. The pair were later identified as David Deshazo and his fiancée, Roxanna Latham. Further

Dr William Bass (right) stands with field officers at the scene of a crime. His pioneering work at 'the body farm' (the Anthropology Research Facility at the University of Tennessee, Knoxville) has helped immeasurably in the fight against crime

investigation revealed that the pair had moved to Henry County, and were living only two miles away from where the body was found. (McLendon's apartment was over two hundred miles away from the scene of the crime.)

The case goes cold

The circumstances linking Deshazo and Latham to the murder certainly looked suspicious, and detectives did their best to follow up the various leads in the case and find more evidence so that the suspects could be charged, but in the end they were unable to do so. There was nothing more concrete to link the pair to the crime and the case eventually went cold.

However, there still remained hope that somehow, this case could be solved – there was just too much evidence to simply forget about it. Then one of the investigators had the idea of getting in touch with Dr William Bass of the Anthropology Research Facility at the University of Tennessee, Knoxville. Bass was the pioneer of a method of analysing the decomposition of human bodies so that more could be found out about how they died. In particular, he had developed systems for studying the way insects devour the human body, paying attention to the time scale of their activity so that the exact moment that the victim died could be calculated. This important, useful, but rather gruesome work earned the Research Facility the nickname of 'The Body Farm' when it was described in a book by best-selling novelist, Patricia Cornwell.

Measuring maggots

Dr Bass began his research on the McLendon body by analysing photographs of it, taken when it was first found in the furniture dump. By looking at the way it had decomposed, he was able to estimate that McLendon had died on 27 September 1992 or before. He was certain that McLendon had not been killed after that date. However, this information was not precise enough for the investigators. McLendon had disappeared almost a week before the twenty-seventh, and the police needed to know exactly when.

Accordingly, Dr Bass looked into the case once again, and this time came up with more detailed information. He studied the photographs of the body once more, and measured the size of the maggots that had infested it. He then found weather reports for the month of September 1992 and, through assessing and analysing the size of the maggots in combination with the climate temperature, calculated that the victim had most probably died on 21 September or the following day.

The killers found

While Dr Bass was studying the remains of Jerry McLendon, police detectives had reopened their investigation. This time, they found more to go on. Deshazo and Latham were no longer on good terms, and Latham now gave evidence against her former boyfriend. She said that she had come upon Deshazo killing McLendon in his flat, suffocating him with a pillow in a fit of jealousy, and had then become so afraid of her boyfriend that she did whatever he told her. In this way,

she was forced to steal from McLendon's bank account, and to help throw his body on the furniture tip.

Detectives asked Latham to call Deshazo on the phone, and as the conversation progressed, it became clear that Latham had not been telling the whole truth in her interviews with the police. Deshazo mentioned that Latham had drugged McLendon by tipping a bottle of Xanax (a tranquillizer) into a spaghetti sauce that she had then served up to him. This indicated that she was, from the beginning, involved in the plot to murder McLendon, and was not, as she alleged, forced into it by her boyfriend.

Both suspects were subsequently charged with murder. David Deshazo was convicted of murder in the first degree, while Roxanna Latham gained a verdict of murder in the second degree.

'The Body Farm'

The murder of Jerry McLendon might never have been solved had it not been for the expertise of Dr William Bass and his team at the Body Farm. Bass initially worked for the Smithsonian Institute in Washington DC, studying skeletal remains of Native Americans. He began his forensic work when the Kansas Bureau of Investigation asked him to help in a cattle-rustling case, by looking at the bones of a cow to see exactly when it had died. When he was unable to find any case studies, he came up with the idea of killing a cow and studying the decomposition of the body under rigorous scientific conditions. His planned experiment never took place, but when he moved to Knoxville, Tennessee, and began to work with the police there, he thought of the idea again – but this time, with a difference.

He figured that, in a more populated area, dead bodies would be found before they became skeletons. Because of this, in order to assess the time of death, it would be necessary to look at insect infestation of the body, rather than at the bones. The only way to do this scientifically would be to lay bodies out on a plot of land and watch them decompose, making notes and studying the exact times that insects such as flies and beetles began to get to work on them. It sounded like a strange idea, but Bass was convinced his method would work. He eventually gained permission from the authorities to use a plot of land for this purpose, and was also able to take possession of some corpses which had been unclaimed from the morgue. (Today, many people leave their bodies in their will to the Body Farm, to be used for the purposes of aiding law enforcement.)

Odours and insects

Bass set up his 'Body Farm', as it came to be known, with a team of researchers from the university. They found that as a corpse rots, it begins to give off chemicals that flies are able to smell from a long way off, in some cases from several miles away. Then, as more chemicals are emitted, other insects come to the scene. When the flies hatch their eggs, ants eat them; when the maggots are born, beetles do the same. Spiders and moths also infest the body. The maggots that survive their predators then begin to eat the body, a process that lasts for two weeks. When the maggots depart, they leave a trail behind them. Nature's predator timetable provides the clue to how long the corpse has been there.

By studying all this insect activity, in minute detail, Bass and his team found it possible to make far more accurate estimations of a body's time of death than had hitherto been possible. For this reason, his work became extremely useful in helping police investigations, and was used in a number of cases. As well as the Jerry McLendon case, there were others, including that of a Mississippi family whose bodies were found in their house in December 1993. Through the research team's work, detectives were able to place the time of death at a month before the discovery of the victims' bodies and, armed with this knowledge, were able to charge a suspect with the murder. The suspect, a relative, was later convicted of the crime.

Studying insects finally led to the solving of the Jerry McLendon murder, and helped a myriad more other crimes on the police's cold case files.

COLD CASES: ACROSS AMERICA

IN MANY CASES OF MURDER, THE KILLER IS UNKNOWN - AT LEAST INITIALLY - AND MUST BE PURSUED BY THE FORCE OF LAW UNTIL HE OR SHE IS FOUND. BUT IN AN UNUSUAL CASE THAT OCCURRED IN AUSTIN, TEXAS, IT WAS THE VICTIM, AS WELL AS THE MURDERER, WHO WAS A MYSTERY.

One of the most challenging cases on the files of the Austin Police Department Cold Case Unit concerned a murder dating more than twenty years ago. On a Saturday night in August 1985, a witness named Dion Garcia saw a murder occur in the city. He heard shouts, and looked out of his window to see two men fighting each other in the front yard of the house next door. One of the men then rushed into the house to get a club, and when he came out, began to beat the other man until he fell over. After that, he pulled out a knife and stabbed him to death.

When the police were called, they could not identify the victim. They released a composite sketch of him, hoping that someone would recognize it and contact the authorities. They also found out that his first name was Jaime. But no one came forward, and the victim remained unknown for the next twenty years.

Then one day, Jose Flores-Salas, who had been detained in custody in Canada, confessed to the murder. In response, the Austin Police Department travelled to Canada to talk to him and found out more details of what had

The proximity of Texas to Mexico means that their police's crime cases will involve Hispanic people. There can be no doubt that some years ago these cases counted for less than those involving more affluent people, and this led to a marked number of cold cases in this ethnic group

happened. They tracked down Jaime's family, who filled in the rest of the story.

It turned out that the parents had thought their son, Jaime Guajardo Hilario, had forgotten about them. As a youngster, he had dreamed of a better life, and had promised to keep in touch when he left home to seek fame and fortune in the big city. However, the family had never heard from him again. His brother-in-law said: 'Twenty years ago his dream was to have money and a good life. We thought he had success and forgot about us.' He went on, 'There was a time that I felt anger because he forgot about his mom. Now things are different. Jaime is no longer with us. He's waiting for us in another world.'

A confession after twenty years by Jose Flores-Salas meant Jaime's case could finally be marked 'Solved'

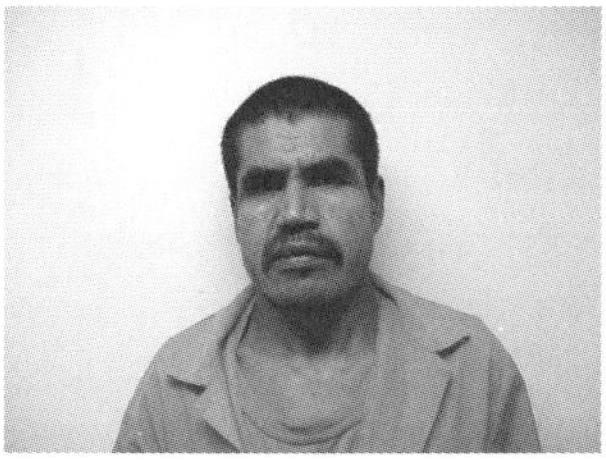

As a result of the police investigations into the case, twenty

The composite sketch of Jaime Guajardo Hilario that was released at the time of his murder. It gave the police the victim's first name to go on, but not much else

years after his death, the body of Jaime Guajardo Hilario was brought back to Saltillo to be buried next to his father in the graveyard. This was hardly a happy ending to the story, but as the Austin Police Department pointed out, it showed that the cold case unit would go to every length to solve the cases of every victim on their books, regardless of their race or nationality.

Miami

Miami is well known as a city where drug dealing is a constant problem for law enforcement agencies. It is also well known that much of the drug running activity involves violent crime. The case of James Larkins was one such crime. But although police detectives knew that Larkins was a cocaine dealer, they could not find out any more about him: no one who knew anything about the case wanted to take their story to the police; for fear that their own illegal activities would be uncovered. Thus, the case mouldered on police shelves until, fifteen years later, the murder was solved.

It was March 1985 when James Larkins, a thirty-year-old cocaine dealer, was shot dead in his car. Police knew that he was part of an underworld of drugs and vice, but they were unable to penetrate the conspiracy of silence that surrounded the murder. It was only when two of Larkins' associates were picked up for unrelated crimes that the names of Larkins' killers came to light. The police promised that the courts would give the men lighter sentences if they revealed

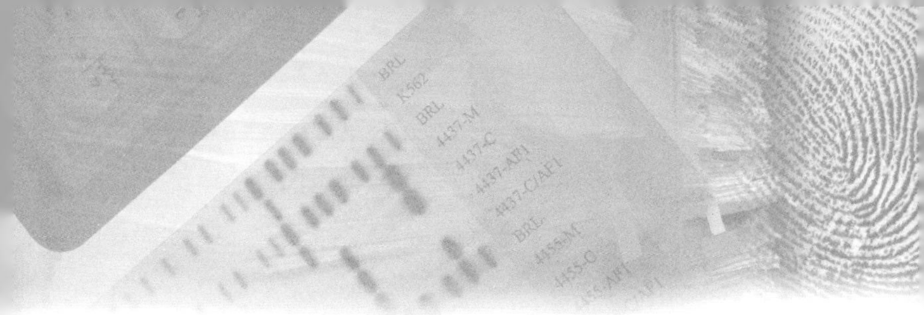

who had committed the murder, and in this way, obtained the information. It had taken fifteen years to find out who had murdered Larkins, but in the end, the killer became known. As police detective Gary Smith, supervisor of the Miami-Dade Cold Case Squad remarked, 'Over time, people's relationships with each other change. Friends are no longer friends. People divorce. They might find religion. So those people who didn't give information before might now be willing.'

Sometimes it is only the passage of time, and people's consequent changes in loyalties and interests, that warms up a cold case and makes it possible to solve a murder. Thus, detectives working in cold case squads often find it useful, when they reopen a case after a number of years, to go back and interview family, friends, and business associates once more, just in case things have changed and someone now wants to tell the truth about a person they might once, before, have protected.

Sacramento

In Sacramento, California, a new training programme for police officers has been set up, which specializes in cold case investigations. It has long been recognized that people often commit crimes when they are young that they later come to regret. A call of conscience and new, more sober moral values may encourage former criminals to come forward and tell the truth about the past. According to Sergeant Bill Tanton, a consultant for the California Cold Case Investigation Course, 'We find time has been an ally. Particularly in gang-related cases, a lot of these young kids have changed their minds and grown up and realized what they were involved in.'

Time has also helped in another way, with advances in DNA profiling, which has revolutionized the investigation of cold cases. Today, just by feeding information into a computer, it is sometimes possible to score a hit and identify a killer. A computerized national database named CODIS now stores DNA profiles taken from samples of known felons in the United States. According to Sharon

Pagaling Hagan, whose full-time job consists in working on criminal investigation profiles for the state of California, 'DNA is so sophisticated now, just in the last few years we've been able to move from saying it's one in ten thousand people to saying, this is the only person on the face of the earth that will have this DNA profile. Obviously, it changes everything.'

Nevada

In September 1977, a six-year-old girl named Lisa Marie Bonham went missing while visiting relatives in Reno, Nevada. She was at an amusement park and left her brother to get a dollar from her parents to go on another ride. She was never seen again. Later, her clothes were found in Toiybe National Forest, Nevada.

At the time, it was not possible to make a DNA profile, because the technology needed to do so was not widely available. However, detectives kept her clothing, and many years later, the blood found on it was analysed and tested. A DNA profile was obtained, and was fed into the Crime Laboratory at the Washoe County Sheriff's office. A match was made to the DNA profile of a man named Stephen Robert Smith, a 57-year-old man who had been paroled since his release from prison in 1976. He had served a prison sentence for sexually molesting two young girls. He was arrested and charged with the murder. When the case was brought to trial, he was found guilty, and was sent back behind bars. Twenty-three years after the murder, the case was finally closed.

Richmond, Virginia

DNA profiling also helped to solve a baffling case of rape and homicide that occurred in Richmond, Virginia, in 1994. The victim had been found in her apartment, and samples of semen and blood had been taken from the body, but despite this, the police were unable to find a suspect for the murder. As a result, the case went cold, until in 1998, when a DNA profile was made from the samples, and routinely fed into the national CODIS database. To the surprise of

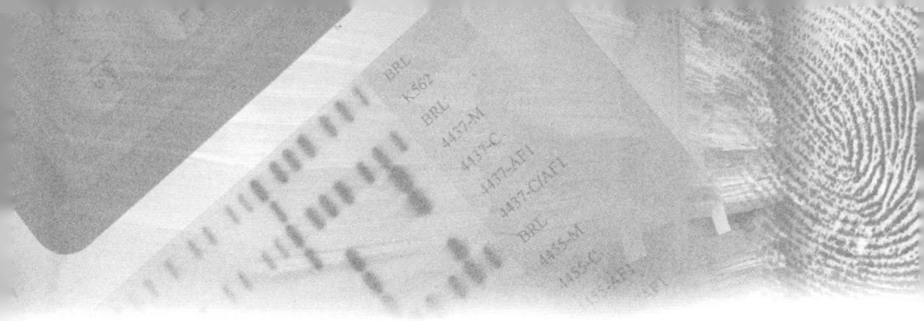

the police department, the DNA profile matched that of a twenty-year-old prisoner, who was serving a sentence for another rape and murder. In this way, the case was reopened once more – this time, with a very clear indication as to who the killer was.

San Diego

DNA profiling is not the only method used by police criminal investigation teams in solving cold cases today. In modern times, the media also plays an increasingly important role in murder investigations. For example Sergeant Jorge Duran, Supervisor of the San Diego Cold Case Unit, has explained how he used the media to close an old unsolved case that had perplexed the police for many years. It concerned one Gilberto Araiza, who, along with an accomplice, fatally stabbed a city shuttle bus driver in 1983.

The accomplice later told police that Araiza was the perpetrator of the crime, whereupon Araiza went into hiding in Mexico. There he remained until the year 2000, when a Latin American television station ran a feature on him. The show was called *Primer Impacto*, and was similar in format to the well-known *America's Most Wanted*. It was not long before the station received a call concerning the item, and referred the caller to the San Diego Cold Case Unit. Araiza was found, arrested, and brought to trial for the murder. He was convicted, and today is serving a term of life imprisonment without possibility of parole.

Sergeant Duran explains that, in many instances, detectives working on cold cases such as these develop a strong desire to see justice done, out of a sense of obligation to the victims and their families, whom they often work very closely with and get to know very well. 'On some occasions, the investigator gets to know a lot about the victim by interviewing their friends and family,' Duran comments. 'And he gets a sense of wanting to bring this to a close because this person didn't deserve this.'

FRANK BENDER: FORENSIC SCULPTURE TO SOLVE CRIME

THE CASE OF JOHN LIST HAS BECOME FAMOUS AS AN EXAMPLE OF A CRIME SOLVED BY A PARTICULAR TYPE OF FORENSIC INVESTIGATION - SCULPTURE. THE PIONEER OF THIS METHOD OF DETECTION IS FRANK BENDER, AN ARTIST WITH AN UNCANNY ABILITY TO VISUALIZE WHAT A CRIMINAL - OR VICTIM - MIGHT LOOK LIKE.

Working with any clue he can find, from the remains of a mangled, decomposed body to an out-of-date photograph, Bender is able to build up a visual profile of his subject with amazing accuracy. Using a mixture of technical information and artistic instinct, he builds a sculpture of the subject and photographs it. The image of the head is then broadcast on television and pictured in the press so that members of the public may come forward with information. In this way, several dangerous criminals have been brought to justice, sometimes after many years of being on the run, and the files on many other wanted criminals constantly updated and revised.

Murdered one by one

One of the most successful of Bender's assignments was the case of John List.

The face of 1970s America: no-one could have guessed the horrifying crime that was to be perpetrated on this family by John List, father and husband

List was born in Bay City, Michigan on 17 September 1925. The only child of Lutheran parents, List grew up under the watchful eye of a controlling mother, attending church regularly and leading Sunday school sessions. During the Second World War, he joined the army, and later qualified as an accountant. However, he did not get on well with his colleagues, earning a reputation as a loner, and his lack of empathy caused constant problems in his career. Nevertheless, he married, raised a family, and lived in an expensive home. To the casual observer, he looked like a successful man.

In reality, however, his life was a mess. His wife was suffering from mental illness, and he was having difficulty paying the bills for extravagant items he had bought for the house, such as a Tiffany glass ceiling. He was plagued by guilt, feeling that his career failures had let his family down. He was also anxious about his daughter, who was interested in pursuing a career as an actress, an activity he considered deeply evil. As he explained later to his pastor in a letter, he was overcome by the need to save his family's souls, so that they would not be corrupted by the sinful modern world.

List eventually decided to murder each of them, one by one, laying them out on sleeping bags and praying over them before he left the house. The bodies were not discovered until one month later, by which time List had disappeared and begun his new life as a fugitive.

America's Most Wanted

Police investigating the murder followed up hundreds of leads at the time, but to no avail. However, eighteen years later the List case was unearthed and became the subject of the television show *America's Most Wanted*. It was the oldest, coldest case ever to be featured on the show, and the producers were aware that the murderer, wherever he was, would by now look very different. The producers asked forensic artist Frank Bender to help.

As always, Bender took great care with his research. By looking at photographs of List's parents, as well as List himself, he was able to predict how the murderer would have aged. He also analysed the case with criminal psychologist John Walter, building up a picture of List's personality, particularly as it would relate to his current appearance.

Rigid habits

Together, Bender and Walter came up with a picture of List's way of life after the murders. Because List was a man with rigid habits, they predicted that he would

Hardly the face of a criminal: Frank Bender achieved an uncanny likeness of the suspect using his skill as a sculptor and clever techniques of character analysis

move, but not too far away, and that he would marry an easily dominated woman. They thought he would become a member of a Lutheran church, continue to work as an accountant, and still be in debt. They imagined that he would dress conventionally and still wear glasses, as he had done at the time of the murders, rather than changing to contact lenses, which were now available. Bender intuited, however, that List would by now have changed the style of the glasses, wearing ones with thick, heavy rims designed to make the wearer look serious and intelligent.

It also seemed likely, from the research they conducted, that List would have done very little, other than change his name, to disguise his identity. List had a scar behind his right ear but probably would not have had cosmetic surgery to cover this up. John List was at heart an unimaginative man who would simply try to forget the past and resume his routine as quickly as possible somewhere else, without taking too much trouble to cover his tracks.

The need to do good

Using this information, Bender built a clay bust of List, adding each detail, such as his hair and glasses, with infinite care. When the clay bust was shown on television, a former neighbour of List's immediately recognized and identified him. The FBI followed up the lead, and on 1 June 1989, ten days after the call, List

It also seemed likely, from the research they conducted, that List would have done very little, other than change his name, to disguise his identity.

was arrested. He was now living under the name Bob Clark, but – as Bender had predicted – other than that, had done little to disguise his identity. Amazingly enough, all Bender's other predictions were proved right too. List was living less than three hundred miles from his former home, had remarried, was working as an accountant, and still had financial difficulties. He dressed conservatively and had changed to the exact same style of heavy-framed glasses that Bender had added to the clay bust.

John List was taken into police custody and charged with five murders: of his mother, his wife, and his three children. The following year, on 1 May 1990, he was convicted of all the murders, and sentenced to life imprisonment five times over. He expressed no regret for his crimes.

Today, Frank Bender continues to work as a forensic sculptor and has helped to provide information on many other criminal investigations. Often working on horrifying cases, using body parts and other clues to build up a visual profile of his subjects, he continues to be committed to his work, saying, 'It's the need to do good and help cut the cancer out of society, and to find truth. I felt that from the very first case.'

John List in 1989, listening as his bail is set at $5 million. Seventeen years after committing his heinous crime, he was given five life sentences

NECROSEARCH: USING ALL FIELDS OF CRIME FIGHTING

EIGHTEEN YEARS IS A LONG TIME FOR A MURDER CASE TO REMAIN UNSOLVED. FOR THE MOTHER OF 25-YEAR-OLD MICHELLE WALLACE, IT WAS TOO LONG - SHE COMMITTED SUICIDE WHEN THE SUSPECT WHO WAS PICKED UP FOR HER MURDER WAS RELEASED FOR LACK OF EVIDENCE TO BRING A CHARGE. YET MANY YEARS LATER, THE SAME SUSPECT WAS ARRESTED AGAIN, AND THIS TIME, DID NOT ESCAPE THE LAW. HAD SHE WAITED, MICHELLE'S MOTHER MIGHT HAVE SEEN HER DAUGHTER'S KILLER BROUGHT TO JUSTICE - AN EVENT THAT MIGHT HAVE HELPED TO BRING HER SOME CONSOLATION IN HER TRAGIC LOSS.

The murder dates back to 1974, when Michelle Wallace went hiking in Gunnison, Colorado. A photographer, she always took her camera with her wherever she went. When she did not return from her trip, her family contacted the police, who immediately suspected a drifter named Roy Melanson, who had been seen in the area and, as it transpired, was wanted on a rape charge in Texas. He was called in for questioning, and in what seemed like a damning piece of evidence, was found to have possession of Michelle's camera. However, he insisted that, on his travels, he had struck up a friendship with the young woman, and that she had given him the camera as a gift. This seemed unlikely, but there was no further evidence to link him to Michelle's disappearance, and there was not enough evidence to charge him. Disappointed, the police let him go, aware that there was more to the story than Melanson had told them, but

Unlike criminals, the camera never lies: Michelle Wallace was a keen photographer – her camera was found in the possesion of her murderer

unable to make any further progress in the case. In a shocking reaction to this, Michelle's mother then committed suicide, unable to bear the situation of not knowing what had happened to her beloved daughter.

Human hair and scalp found

The next piece of evidence to turn up in the Wallace case came from some hikers, who found a scrap of human scalp and a lock of brown hair in a remote part of

The beautiful Beckwith mountains in Colorado are a popular place for hikers as they are wild and uninhabited – but this meant that there was no-one around to witness Michelle's death

the Gunnison area. Encouraged by this find, investigators doubled their efforts to find Wallace's body and combed the area, but to no avail. The young woman had apparently disappeared without trace. Eventually, all the leads on the case ran out and Michelle's file was left to gather dust on the shelf.

It was not until 1992 that the case was reopened as the result of a new initiative, Necrosearch International. This organization was formed in 1991 by a group of experts in various fields, including chemistry, geology, biology, and anthropology, who wanted to use their expertise to help solve crime, in particular by helping to locate human remains and other hidden evidence in murder cases. Working separately and as a group, they try to analyse all aspects of a case and then put them together to see if any new evidence can be turned up. In the case of Michelle Wallace, they were able to do so.

First, twenty of the group members mapped out a grid to cover the Gunnison area where the scalp and hair fragment had been found. Their aim was to comb every inch of the terrain, so that nothing could be missed. Using a combination of sharp-eyed observation, expert training in a wide variety of academic

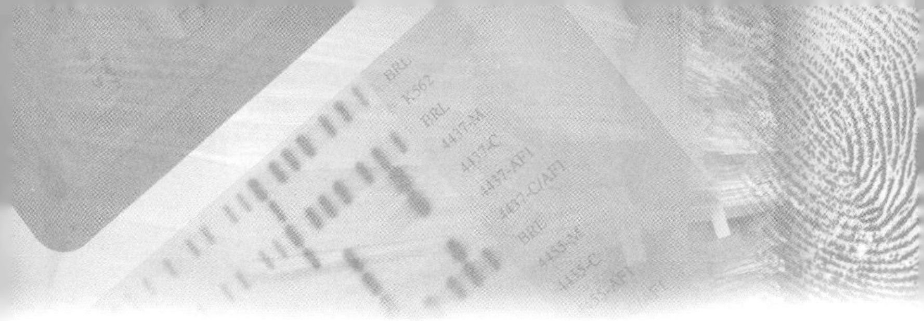

disciplines, and in some cases high-tech electronic equipment, they walked through the area they had mapped, each aligned at an arm's length from the other.

The gold tooth

The break came when Cecilia Travis, a geologist, noticed what she at first thought was a large white mushroom. However, she noticed something unusual: there appeared to be something within it, gleaming in the sun. She went to take a closer look, and found that the object she had taken to be a mushroom was, in fact, a skull with a gold tooth still in it. The team then dug up the nearby area and found bones buried there.

The skull and its gold tooth were later compared with dental X-rays of the victim and confirmed as belonging to Michelle Wallace. Roy Melanson was arrested, and this time he was not released. He was charged with the murder of Michelle Wallace and brought to trial, where he was found guilty and sentenced to life imprisonment.

For Michelle's mother, it was, tragically, too late. For her father, who had lost both his wife and his daughter because of Melanson, justice had been a long time in coming, but in the end it came, and he was able at least to know that his daughter's killer was behind bars at last.

She went to take a closer look, and found that the object she had taken to be a mushroom was, in fact, a skull with a gold tooth still in it.

Necrosearch

Necrosearch, the team that found the body of Michelle Wallace, is a fascinating organization that brings together the skills of a variety of academics and specialists in different fields, for the purpose of finding clandestine gravesites. Their avowed aim is to assist law enforcement agencies in their work, by providing research, training, and on-site investigations. None of the members of the organization is paid, and all work is done on a voluntary basis. The organization also provides training courses in specialist subject areas for their highly educated members, who are also screened by police to make sure their interest is genuine.

A glance at the list of Necrosearch's members reveals just how technically skilled their members are, and how much knowledge goes into making discoveries such as that of Wallace's body. For example, there are individuals who study the behaviour of animal scavengers such as bears, foxes, coyotes and birds, which attack human remains in the wild, often moving them around to different sites. Then there are anthropologists who study the remains themselves, especially bones, to find out whether these are indeed human rather than animal remains. Archaeologists help to reconstruct the events in a crime, such as burial; botanists study vegetation to find out about such features as disturbances in the earth's surface; entomologists look at insect activity on cadavers; geologists note intrusions into the natural environment; and meteorologists chart climactic changes. Meanwhile, geophysicists use remote sensors, such as radar, electromagnetics, thermal imaging, and metal detectors to locate clandestine graves. More old-fashioned, but no less effective, is the work of experienced dog handlers, who use bloodhounds to help in this endeavour, and professional divers, who are able to search underwater sites where necessary.

In this way, Necrosearch has coordinated investigations in a way that would never be possible using police resources only, and come up with a great deal of useful information for homicide investigators in the state of Colorado and elsewhere – all completely free of charge.

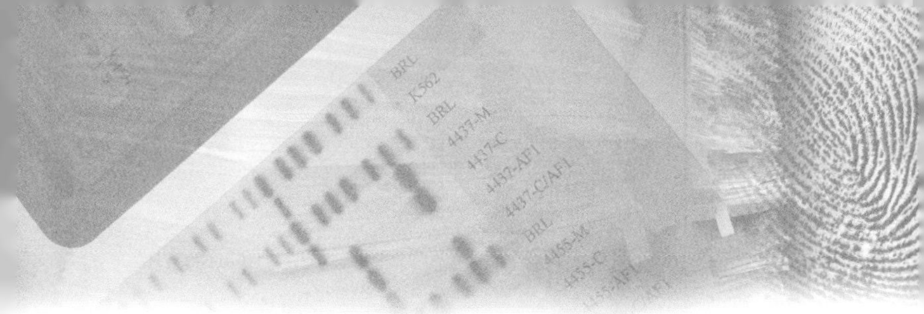

OPERATION PHOENIX: HOPE FROM THE COLD ASHES OF DESPAIR

POLICE FORCES OFTEN HAVE EVIDENCE AT THEIR DISPOSAL THAT IS YEARS, EVEN DECADES OLD. IN MANY INSTANCES, IT HAS BEEN COLLECTED FROM THE SCENE OF A CRIME THAT TOOK PLACE WHEN TECHNIQUES FOR ANALYSIS OF DNA WERE NOT AS ADVANCED AS THEY ARE NOW. THIS EVIDENCE CAN NOW BE REVIEWED, RE-ANALYSED AND MATCHED WITH OTHER INFORMATION, SO THAT UPDATED PROFILES CAN BE OBTAINED, LEADING TO THE IDENTIFICATION AND ARREST OF A CRIMINAL.

One pioneering team that has solved a number of crimes in this way is Operation Phoenix, Britain's largest cold case review centre. Run by the Northumbria Police Force in the north of England, Operation Phoenix was set up in February 2002 to look at rape and sexual assault crimes, some of which took place over twenty years ago. According to this scheme, DNA profiles are obtained and then loaded into a database which contains police files on serial offenders in sexual assault cases. If the DNA profiles match up, the case can be reopened and re-investigated, often with surprising results.

A twist of fate

The idea of revisiting violent crimes in this way came from a report into the murder of Stephen Lawrence, a black teenager who was killed in a racist attack in London in 1993. Although such attacks had happened before, the lack of police response

in this case provoked a national outcry. A public inquiry in 1997 eventually found that the police were guilty of racism. The report made many recommendations, including that the police should reopen unsolved cases wherever possible, instead of allowing them to be filed away as Stephen's had been.

In response, police in Northumbria decided to review all unsolved rape and sexual assault cases dating from the mid 1980s, using new forensic techniques to gain genetic profiles of criminals and match them with a national DNA database. They named the initiative Operation Phoenix.

The results of the operation were extraordinary, far exceeding expectations, and led to the conviction of many violent rapists and sexual offenders who terrorized their communities for years. The success of Operation Phoenix also led the way for many other police services in Europe and the United States, who are now beginning to adopt a similar approach: using forensics in combination with police files to warm up cold cases and solve 'unsolvable' crimes. Through matching DNA samples, often from patches of blood or sweat that are decades old, police have tracked down criminals and proved their guilt beyond doubt.

Not just murderers

Evidence from paedophile victims is, in particular, reviewed, and this led to the arrest and conviction of Alan Chater. In 1996, Chater had accosted two young children playing near their homes and asked them to help him find his wallet in bushes. Once in the bushes, he had indecently assaulted them, threatening them with a knife. Four years later, he had struck again, this time assaulting two young boys and a child aged only three. At the time, police took samples from the scenes of the crimes, including evidence from the children's clothing, but it was only after several more years had elapsed that these could be used to build a DNA profile of the attacker.

When Chater's profile, obtained from the samples, was loaded into the police database on suspected paedophiles, a match was found. The case on Chater,

The five youths charged with – but never convicted of – the murder of Stephen Lawrence run the gauntlet of an angry crowd as they leave a Public Inquiry, June 1998

then aged fifty-four, was reopened and he was re-investigated, eventually being charged with the crimes. He pleaded guilty and was convicted.

Other cases included the rape of an eleven-year-old girl, who was waiting at a bus stop in November 1981. The child was dragged off and raped, in a terrifying ordeal that shocked the local community. Police were under intense pressure to find the culprit and spent months sifting through information, but in the end the case went completely cold and was filed away. Twenty-three years later, however, Operation Phoenix reopened it, using DNA profiling to identify, charge and convict Ernest John Wallace. Wallace, who had also committed a similar offence in 1977, was given a fifteen-year prison sentence.

Operation Phoenix is now regarded as one of the most successful and far-reaching police operations in Europe.

COLD SWEAT

The advent of DNA technology has created a revolution in the solving of cold cases. Today, with DNA profiling, the police and legal authorities have a very powerful tool in their possession – a system of identification that is almost always entirely correct. As a result, in the twenty-first century, all over the country, specialist police units are being formed to deal with the backlog of unsolved cases on their files – cases that can now be reviewed in the light of this new technology. Their task is immense, but theoretically at least, it may be possible for them to solve many old, cold cases purely through computer analysis.

CODIS is a national database which aims to list the DNA profile of every convicted felon in America. When a murder, rape, or other violent crime is committed, samples of blood, semen, hair, and so on can be taken from a victim's body, and the results analysed to create a DNA profile. This profile is then fed into the computer, in the hopes that a match will be made against the database. To date, this system has been very effective; all the cases in this section, and indeed, a large number of the cold cases described in this book as a whole, have been solved in this way.

05

FARYION WARDRIP: THE SILVER-TONGUED PREACHER

TERRY SIMS WAS FOUND DEAD IN HER APARTMENT IN WICHITA FALLS, TEXAS, IN THE DECEMBER OF 1984. THE NEXT SPRING, THE NAKED BODY OF TONI GIBBS WAS FOUND LYING IN A SCRUB-BRUSH FIELD BY AN ELECTRICIAN CHECKING A MALFUNCTIONING TRANSFORMER, AND IN THE LATE SUMMER OF THAT SAME YEAR, THE NAKED CORPSE OF ELLEN BLAU WAS DISCOVERED IN A DITCH BY A COUNTY EMPLOYEE MOWING THE VERGES OF A COUNTRY ROAD.

Sims' murder was investigated by the Wichita Falls City Police. Gibbs' body was discovered a stone's throw over the county line, and was investigated by the Archer County Sheriff's Department. Blau was found outside the city limits, and the murder was investigated by the local sheriff.

Three dead bodies and three different law enforcement agencies. None of them shared notes or other information, nor did they pool resources and work collectively. The murders were not seen as being related and each agency had their own suspect. The city police thought Sims' killer was a co-worker; in Archer County they believed that Gibbs was murdered by her admirer Danny Laughlin. The Wichita Falls sheriff focused his attentions on Blau's former boyfriend. Of the three suspects, only Laughlin was ever charged, and a jury acquitted him eleven to one. The three cases went cold. It was years later before anyone realized that they might have been connected.

Bricklayer turns sleuth

John Little had always wanted to be a policeman, but he failed the medical due to poor eyesight. Instead he went into construction, and gained a reputation as an adept and reliable bricklayer – although his heart was never in it. After several attempts he succeeded in realizing his dream in 1993, and became part of the District Attorney's investigative team.

Faryion Wardrip, a non-descript looking man: a fact that helped protect him as people found him to be likable and trustworthy

It was December 1998, almost fourteen years to the day after Terry Sims was murdered, when DA Barry Macha admitted to Little that he had come to see the three unsolved murders as a stain on his career. He asked Little to look into it. Perhaps something had been missed.

For John Little, it was not just a regular investigation. He could remember the night he found out Toni Gibbs had gone missing. He remembered telling his wife, who had been friends with Gibbs at college. When the police asked for volunteers to help the search parties he had stepped forward, and brought his brother with him. They had spent the whole day on foot, a silent group of solemn strangers, their eyes peeled to the ground, braced for the worst. But they had found nothing. Eventually, several weeks later an electrician had stumbled upon Gibbs' corpse in the course of a routine repair.

Although Little never told Bracha this, the murders had never been far from his mind. Over the years he had found himself taking solitary drives to sites that were connected with them, hoping something might jog his memory, or get him thinking. Now that he was on the case, it was plain old diligence that got him on the right track. Little went through the three files and made lists of every name that came up or could come up in each one, and then compared lists to see if any of

them reappeared. One name came up three times, and after a brief records check, the former bricklayer knew he was onto something.

The preacher with a past

Faryion Wardrip was living in Olney, Texas, when John Little made the connection. He had gained a reputation as a conscientious worker and taught Sunday school at his local chapel. A well-known figure in the parish, he hoped to begin training as a Baptist preacher. But Wardrip was a preacher with a past. If you looked closely, you could see an electronic monitoring bracelet around his ankle. Clearly, Wardrip was on parole for a serious crime. If parishioners asked, he usually told them he had been serving a manslaughter sentence for killing his girlfriend in a drink-driving accident. Sometimes he would say he got into a bar-room brawl and ended up killing a man. As his family would later put it, 'Faryion is one of those people who would climb a tree to tell a lie when it was just as easy to stand on the ground and tell the truth.' Even in his youth in Marion, Indiana, where he was a high school dropout, Wardrip had lied about himself extensively. Later, he would boast about the glory of his military days, although the truth was that he had been discharged from the army for drug use.

But as it turned out, Wardrip really did have something to hide. He had been convicted in 1986 of murdering a female friend, Tina Kimbrew, and sentenced to thirty-five years.

Kimbrew's parents had campaigned to secure a life sentence, but the Texas Department of Criminal Justice had launched a new Victim Offender Dialogue programme, and the family was asked if they wanted to participate. The idea was to give a victim's family an opportunity to question the criminal who had killed their loved one, about their reasons; about the crime; about anything. Wardrip, who claimed to have found God while he was behind bars, was keen to get talking.

After a five-hour session, Robert Kimbrew was so convinced that Wardrip was full of remorse, that his opinions changed. 'When you get out of here,' he said to

Tagged but unrepentent: by apparently turning to God, Wardrop literally talked his way out of jail – allowing him to rape and murder again

the supposedly penitent Wardrip, 'if you find yourself headed for trouble again, and you run out of other people to turn to for help, you can call me.' Thanks in no small part to the results of this new dialogue programme, Wardrip was paroled in 1993. Tina's father had expressed admirable Christian sentiments, but he was wrong about Wardrip. Wardrip had not told him the full story, by any means.

A stolen coffee cup

Semen samples had been collected from the bodies of Terry Sims and Toni Gibbs when their bodies had been autopsied; Ellen Blau's body had been in such a severe state of decomposition when it was found that it offered practically no physical evidence. In a police laboratory archive the samples were kept carefully, until such time as forensic technology would develop to a level where it might become useful. In 1996, DNA profiling became part of the law enforcement programme in Texas. It showed that Gibbs and Sims had been raped (and almost certainly killed) by the same man.

It seemed obvious that a DNA sample from the suspect was the lynchpin upon which a successful prosecution would depend, but for legal reasons, the district attorney argued that simply asking for a sample would be a waste of time. Then again, if the sample had been obtained without the suspect's consent, this might give the defence lawyer a shot at throwing the case out of court. So the detectives had to come up with another plan.

Little trailed Wardrip for weeks, in plain clothes, in a borrowed car. Being careful not to draw attention to himself, he learnt the details of Wardrip's daily routine, even the habits of his second wife. He found out what day the Wardrips did their laundry on, and spent the whole day in the launderette they frequented, washing the same clothes over and over again. That was when he got his chance. The suspect arrived in his car and parked outside, and Little saw that he was finishing a cup of takeaway coffee. Wardrip was about to throw it away. Thinking quickly, the investigator filled his mouth with a wad of chewing tobacco and approached the suspect:

'Do you mind if I have your cup?'

'My cup?'

'Yeah, for a spit cup.'

'Help yourself.'

Their little verbal exchange was a piece of legal chicanery that meant under an

'abandoned interest' law, any samples taken from the cup would be entirely admissible in court. Back in the lab, working on a trace of Wardrip's saliva, everyone awaited the results with some eagerness. Everyone apart from John Little; he was already convinced.

A fifth victim

Armed with a positive DNA match from the saliva, Little collected Wardrip and brought him to the DA's office. It was the day before Wardrip was due to read at church. Wardrip was hopeful at first that the meeting might be about the removal of his surveillance anklet, and he was right, in a sense. He would not need one where he was going.

The police confronted him with the incontrovertible evidence that Little had collected. Within minutes, Wardrip had confessed. While he was not forthcoming on the details, and made a string of excuses for himself, he admitted to the murder of Terry Lee Sims, a twenty-one-year-old student; Toni Gibbs, a twenty-three-year-old general nurse at the hospital where he had once worked; and Ellen Blau, another student, a year older than Sims. Then came a shock: Wardrip added that he would like to confess to the murder of housewife Debra Taylor in Fort Worth in March 1985, a twenty-six-year-old mother of two. The police had never considered him a suspect for this murder.

As the interview concluded, Wardrip was asked for the record, as is routine, if he had been promised anything in return for making his statement.

'Eternal life with God,' was his answer. 'I was promised I wouldn't burn in hell.'

In November 1999 Faryion Wardrip was sentenced to death by lethal injection. He was forty years of age. Whoever or whatever promised him that he would not burn in hell is a matter of speculation, but the promise that he was about to meet his maker cannot have been of much comfort to him, for within months, and perhaps unsurprisingly, he was trying to bring an appeal against the court's decision.

GERALD PARKER: 'THE BEDROOM BASHER'

TODAY, DNA PROFILING IS A POWERFUL METHOD OF IDENTIFYING CRIMINALS, GIVING EVIDENCE THAT IS EXTREMELY RELIABLE, INDEED INCONTROVERTIBLE. BUT, IN ONE CASE, AS WELL AS IDENTIFYING THE PERPETRATOR OF A SERIES OF CRIMES, DNA PROFILING ALSO HELPED TO FREE A MAN WHO WAS WRONGLY JAILED. THROUGH ANALYSIS OF DNA SAMPLES, GERALD PARKER WAS IDENTIFIED AS 'THE BEDROOM BASHER', A SERIAL RAPIST WHO HAD ALSO MURDERED SEVERAL OF HIS VICTIMS; WHILE THE MAN WHO HAD SERVED SIXTEEN YEARS IN PRISON FOR ONE OF HIS CRIMES, KEVIN GREEN, WAS SET FREE.

In 1980, a twenty-two-year-old Marine, Kevin Lee Green, was convicted of second-degree murder. He was alleged to have attacked his twenty-one-year-old wife, Dianne, who was pregnant at the time. The baby was at full term, but Dianne was beaten so badly that it was later born dead. Dianne also suffered brain damage in the attack and was comatose for a month afterwards. When she came round, she had lost her memory, but even so, she was somehow able to identify her husband as her attacker.

On the face of it, there was not much evidence to convict Green, beyond the testimony of his wife, a woman who had suffered mental impairment as a result of the attack. However, this was an emotive case, and there was a great deal of pressure to obtain a conviction, whatever the price. There were indications that Green was innocent, but they were ignored. Before Green's trial, the defence

Kevin Lee Green's wrongful conviction cost him his marriage and sixteen years' freedom. Thankfully, DNA evidence got him released and the true criminal imprisoned

administered a lie detector test, which Green passed. He was adamant that he had not attacked his wife, claiming that at the time the intruder entered the house, he had gone to buy a cheeseburger, and was not there. A counter girl at the place where he had bought the cheeseburger identified him as a customer, and police gave evidence that the burger was still warm when he called them to the house. However, with such a strong allegation against him, supported by his own wife, the jury found Green guilty of the attack. He was convicted of second-degree murder, and went on to serve sixteen years in jail for his supposed crime.

A bolt from the blue

While in prison, Green tried to arrange a DNA test of the semen sample that had been collected from his wife's body at the scene of the crime. He thought – rightly, as it turned out – that this would show him to be innocent. However, the forensic test was extremely costly, and he was unable to afford the fee to have it done. Fortunately, the semen sample was kept safely as part of the evidence of the unsolved crime; a fact that was to prove very important for Green in the future.

While Green was in jail, he and his wife divorced. He continued to maintain that he had had nothing to do with the attack, and that his wife was lying. For this failure to co-operate and 'admit his crime', he had to forego his privileges and serve his full sentence. Yet, he was determined, whatever the personal cost, to maintain his innocence – not only for the sake of his own dignity, but for that of his family and friends.

Then something extraordinary happened, that must have seemed to him like a bolt from the blue. In 1996, the authorities in Orange County sent several DNA profiles to the state laboratory for analysis. They were samples taken from a series of unsolved rape and murder cases, all of them occurring in 1978 and 1979. This series of attacks had terrified women in the county, and the perpetrator had become known as 'The Bedroom Basher'. The authorities were hoping that the samples from the murder victims would match one of those on the national DNA database, which contained DNA samples from convicted felons across America.

The computer matched the 'Bedroom Basher' samples to that of a man named Gerald Parker. By sheer chance, Parker, like Green, was a former Marine. He had been convicted for a number of sex crimes in the 1980s, and was still serving time in jail for a parole violation connected to one of them. When he was charged, Parker confessed to the murders, and also to the beating and rape of Green's wife. Green was immediately freed. The state issued a formal apology to Green, and Superior Court Judge Robert Fitzgerald found him completely innocent of the crime. However, Green's former wife continued to believe that her ex-husband was responsible for the attack. Once exonerated, the ex-Marine corporal went to live with his family in the Midwest and said he did not plan to sue the state for damages resulting from his wrongful conviction. He might have been eligible for parole earlier had he not insisted throughout that he was innocent.

DNA from sperm traces

At the trial in 1998, the jury of nine women and three men were introduced to the then comparatively new technique of 'genetic fingerprinting', as it was called. An analyst at the Orange County sheriff's crime laboratory, Ed Buse, showed the jury blown-up charts of the DNA test results, which looked somewhat like product bar codes. Buse explained to the prosecutor that the black marks on the 'bar codes' showed where matches had been made between Parker's DNA sample and that of one of the murder victims, Kimberly Gaye Rawlins, from Costa Mesa.

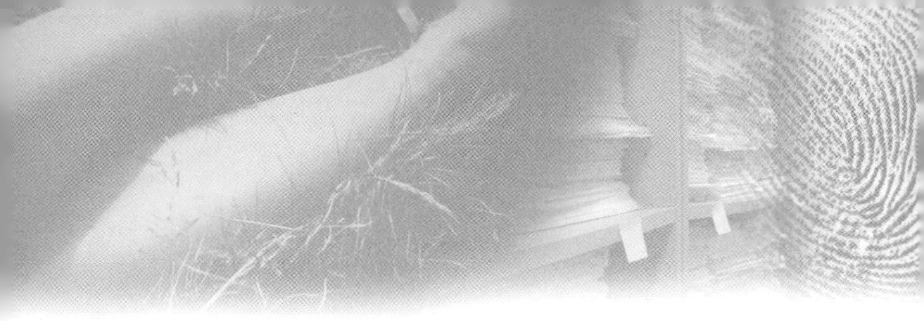

...almost twenty years later... the samples from Rawlins' body could be used in DNA analysis, and were found to match up with Parker's.

Rawlins had been the victim of an attack on 1 April 1979, and had died of multiple skull fractures as a result. She was just twenty-one. After her death, blood and sperm samples had been taken from her body. However, for many years after she was killed, there was no DNA technology available, and the samples had to be stored. Meanwhile, the police had to continue their search for 'the Bedroom Basher' using the normal methods of police investigation. It was not until almost twenty years later that the samples from Rawlins' body could be used in DNA analysis, and were found to match up with Parker's. Buse pointed out that the Rawlins' samples and those from Parker were 'indistinguishable from each other', giving absolutely clear proof that it was Parker who had killed her.

Then Dr Bruce Kovacs, a scientist from the University of Southern California, took the stand to give a general description of DNA, explaining how minute strands of each person's DNA are unique, so that the pinpointing of those strands can distinguish one individual from another (in much the same way – but far more accurately – as the technique of fingerprinting). Dr Kovacs explained how DNA links cells together to form patterns that are unique to each individual, and pointed out that the only people who would share exactly the same DNA would be identical twins. He also described how the technique had been pioneered in the United Kingdom, and used to good order in police work.

Drug and alcohol abuse

In addition to the Rawley murder, Parker was charged with the murder of four other young women: Debra Lynn Senior, Deborah Kennedy, Marolyn Carleton, and Sandra Kay Fry.

Speaking for his client, defence attorney David Zimmerman said that Parker did not dispute the fact that he had committed the murders. However, he alleged that, at the times of the murders, Parker had been suffering from an extremely disturbed state of mind. Parker had also been drunk when he committed the crimes, which, his lawyer argued, ought to lead the jury to convict him of second-degree murder.

While the court proceedings were going on, Parker, now forty-three years old, showed no sign of emotion. He listened to the story of how, as a young Marine, he had been stationed at El Toro Marine Corps Air Station in the late 1970s. There, he had caused panic in the local community by raping and bludgeoning a series of young women to death. He had also been stationed at other Marine bases around the United States, including North Carolina, Alaska and Mississippi, and in 1980 had been convicted of the rape of a thirteen-year-old girl, for which he was serving a prison sentence. He had been due to be released in a matter of weeks. It was thought that Parker may have been responsible for more sex

'We've been waiting a long time for this day. The best day will be in a few years down the line when we're watching him die.'

A miscarriage of justice: unfortunately for Green, his wife's evidence in the court room was enough to put him in jail. Luckily, the physical evidence from the crime scene was kept, and Green was freed as a result of that evidence being matched to Parker

killings, not only in Orange County, but elsewhere in the United States as well.

In Parker's defence, attorney David Zimmerman said that he had a long history of drug and alcohol abuse, and had suffered from mental illness at the time of the murders. Apparently, Parker had since responded well to treatment for psychosis when in prison, and his personality had changed. However, countering Zimmerman, the prosecution insisted that whether or not Parker had changed, he was still responsible for his crimes: he had killed for pleasure, and must now pay the penalty.

Parker responded by saying that he was sorry for the crimes, but his expression remained impassive, even when the judge recommended the death penalty for him. One of the jurors, Nan Smith, commented that Parker's remorse had come 'a little too late', while family and friends of the deceased reacted more strongly. Jackie Bessonnette, whose sister Debra Lynn Senior had been just seventeen when her life was brutally cut short, said, 'We've been waiting a long time for this day. The best day will be a few years down the line when we're watching him die.'

ELAINE GRAHAM: A LONG ROAD TO JUSTICE

THE CASE OF EDMOND JAY MARR IS ONE OF THE MOST EXTRAORDINARY IN THE HISTORY OF THE LOS ANGELES POLICE DEPARTMENT (LAPD). TWENTY YEARS AFTER COMMITTING A MURDER, FOR WHICH HE WAS NOT PUNISHED AT THE TIME, MARR WAS FINALLY TRACKED DOWN. THE DEPARTMENT'S NEW COLD CASE UNIT REOPENED THE FILE ON HIS VICTIM, ELAINE GRAHAM, AND THROUGH ADVANCES IN DNA TECHNOLOGY, WHICH INVOLVED TAKING SAMPLES FROM HER DAUGHTER - A TWO-YEAR-OLD AT THE TIME OF THE MURDER - THIS TIME THEY WERE ABLE TO GAIN A PROFILE OF THE KILLER.

Thus it was that the brutal murder of a young mother was finally avenged, after decades of being just another statistic in the city's roll of violent crimes. Elaine's family and friends thought the authorities had forgotten about her – but they were wrong: they just had to wait a very long time for justice to come their way.

When Elaine Graham met her death, she had everything to live for. She was a hard-working, twenty-nine-year-old nurse with a husband and a young daughter. She had ambitions to become a writer, and was taking writing classes at university. Every night, she wrote a journal in which she addressed her entries to her baby daughter. The night before she was murdered, she wrote an entry about a dream that she had had, in which she and her daughter were a pair of detectives engaged on a case where they caught a bad man and solved a big

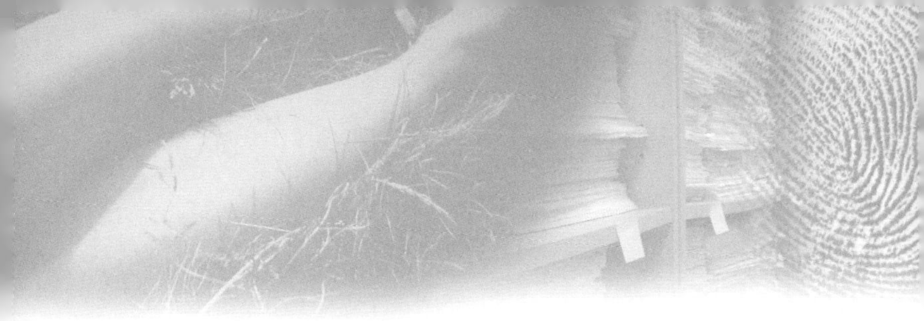

case. The dream was to prove prophetic, but only after years had gone by. And little did Elaine Graham think at the time that it was she herself who would be the victim in the case.

A double-edged dagger

On that fatal morning, 17 March 1983, Graham dropped her daughter off with her carer, and set off to attend her writing class on the campus of the California State University Northridge, which was near her home. That was the last time anyone saw her. She never returned to collect her child that day, and no one knew where she had gone. The police were called in, and next day, in the early hours of the morning, her 1971 Volkswagen was found at a parking lot in the Santa Ana Fashion Square Mall (now known as the Main Place Mall). Detectives from the Robbery and Homicide division of the police department were assigned to the case, and began by focusing their attention on a young man who had been near the Cal State campus on the day that Elaine had disappeared. His name was Edmond Jay Marr.

Marr was twenty-five years old at the time of the investigation. He had just been dishonourably discharged from the army, and was having a difficult time at home, arguing with his parents, especially his father. On the night of the seventeenth, he had visited his sister, who lived only a few blocks away from the mall where Elaine's car was later found. Marr was found in possession of a double-edged dagger. The dagger was taken in for examination, using the conventional techniques of

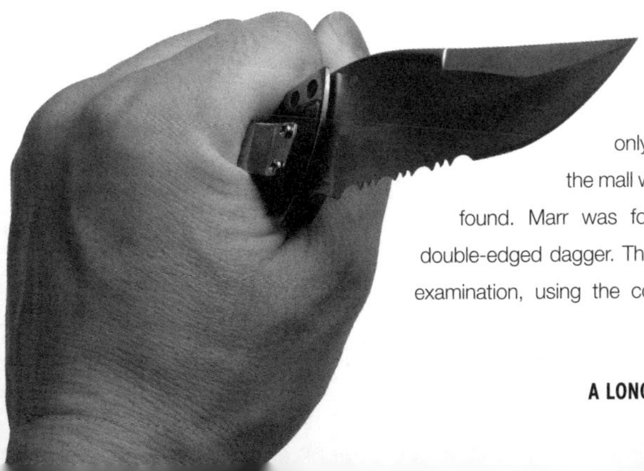

Fitting easily into a pocket, it is all too easy for a murderous urge to be expressed by a knife attack, as Elaine Graham found out to her cost

serology that were available at the time. A tiny patch of blood on the well-cleaned dagger was found that was consistent with the blood type of Elaine Graham, but it was impossible to narrow the match down any further. As the investigation proceeded, it was found that Marr had been arrested for violent robbery, and his dishonourable discharge from the army came to light. However, none of this in itself was concrete enough evidence to charge him with the murder.

Human bones discovered

Eight months later, human bones were discovered by some hikers in Brown's Canyon, a remote area of the hills above Chatsworth. The bones were examined, and it became clear that the victim had met a violent death. There was a dent in one of the rib bones which suggested that the victim had been stabbed. A

The skeleton tells a story: although DNA evidence rarely survives in bone, the bones themselves often retain a good record of how their owner met their death

woman's blouse was also found in the bushes near the bones, and when it was examined, it was noticed that there were no holes in the fabric. The combination of the dent in the bone and the unpunctured fabric of the blouse suggested that the killer had stripped his victim before stabbing her to death.

For Elaine's family, these meagre but horrifying details were all they knew about her last moments. It was a relief for them to know that she had not simply run away and abandoned her dearly loved husband and daughter, but it was deeply traumatic to learn that she had been murdered in such a brutal, terrifying way.

Detectives on the Graham case brought Marr back in for questioning when it was discovered that, as a young man, he had often hiked in the area of Brown's Canyon. The following year, the detectives brought the case to the Los Angeles District Attorney's office, and the decision was made to keep the evidence in the case, including Marr's knife, until advances in forensic technology could give a clearer result. For the time being, despite the new findings, and much to the disappointment of the police officers concerned, there did not seem to be enough evidence to bring the case to the courts.

Sadly, for the next two decades, there were no new leads on the case, and the file on Elaine Graham lay on a shelf in the LAPD's offices. It was not until November 2001 that the case was reviewed, by which time the leading detectives in the investigation, Paul Tippin and Leroy Orozco, had retired from their jobs. In the new millennium, a new unit had now been formed in the Robbery Homicide Division: the Cold Case Homicide Unit. The aim of the unit was to try to solve old, cold cases on the police's files, using the now much improved techniques for DNA profiling. Two new detectives were assigned to the Elaine Graham case: Rick Jackson and Tim Marcia.

Missing piece in the puzzle

Going back through the files, Jackson and Marcia discovered that Marr's dagger had been carefully stored as evidence. Jackson and Marcia ordered the dagger

to be reanalysed by the police forensic department, who re-found the minute amount of blood that had remained underneath its handle. The next step was to obtain a DNA sample from the victim to match it with, so they went to Graham's daughter, Elise. From Elise's DNA, which was the same as her mother's (DNA works in such a way that although there are minute differences between peoples' DNA, these differences are smaller between blood relatives), they matched the blood on the handle. This was something that could not have been done back in 1983, and it was to prove the crucial missing piece in the puzzle of Elaine Graham's death.

As a result of Jackson and Marcia's investigations, which involved witness interviews, phone tap recordings and forensic analysis, Edmond Jay Marr was arrested and charged with the kidnap and murder of Elaine Graham. He was held on a one million dollar bond. His trial received a great deal of publicity, and the courtroom was packed. Friends and relatives of the deceased were there, including one of the detectives who had worked on the case originally in 1983. Graham's daughter Elise, now aged twenty-four, stood up in court and told Marr exactly what losing her mother at such a young age had meant to her. 'You ask this court for mercy,' she said. 'Where was the mercy for my mother? You've given me a life sentence of a broken heart,' she went on. 'You took from me the most important person in the world.' It became clear that, over the twenty years following Graham's death, while the case had gathered dust in terms of the police investigation, there were many for whom it had never grown cold.

Edmond Jay Marr, now forty-seven, pleaded guilty, and admitted the use of a knife in his crime. As a result, his lawyers were able to cut a deal with the prosecution, which resulted in a verdict of second, rather than first-degree murder. He was sentenced by the judge to a prison term of sixteen years.

It had taken twenty years, but in the end, Elaine Graham's prophetic dream had finally come true. She and her daughter Elise had caught a criminal, and solved a case of murder.

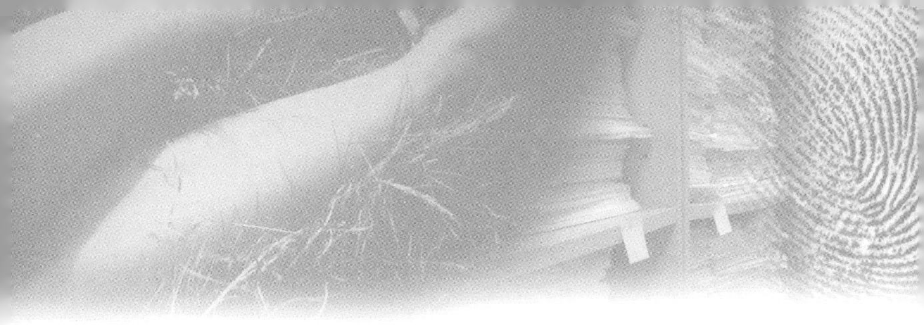

'You ask this court for mercy...Where was the mercy for my mother? You've given me a life sentence of a broken heart.'

A band-aid on a bullet hole?

The case was a triumph for the newly opened unit in the LAPD, which had been criticized in some quarters as 'putting a band-aid on a bullet hole': journalists had pointed out that there were only six detectives and one supervisor assigned to the unit, yet there were over eight thousand unsolved homicide cases on the files for them to deal with, some of which dated as far back as the 1960s. If one calculated that each detective could solve a cold case a month – which was unlikely, given the complications of most criminal investigations – it would take over a century for the team to get up to date. Many felt that public funds would be better spent on detective teams that would solve current crimes, rather than delving into old cases that were unlikely to be resolved.

However, the solving of the Graham case did much to improve the image of the new cold case unit, and it was pointed out that, even if only a few cases were ever solved, this was of crucial importance, not only to the relatives of the victims, but to the morale of the city as a whole. The fact that the unit had been set up, and that there was some impetus towards finding the perpetrators of homicidal crimes, was of great symbolic – if not always literal – significance to the citizens of Los Angeles, in that it showed that the many victims had not been altogether forgotten, and that justice could still be served for at least some of them.

LYNETTE WHITE: VALENTINE'S DAY MASSACRE

THE MURDER OF PROSTITUTE LYNETTE WHITE TOOK PLACE IN CARDIFF, SOUTH WALES, ON ST VALENTINE'S DAY IN 1988. IT BECAME NOTORIOUS FOR TWO REASONS: FIRST, SUCH WAS THE BRUTALITY OF THE CRIME THAT THE POLICE MOUNTED THE BIGGEST MURDER SEARCH EVER TO TAKE PLACE IN WALES; AND SECOND, THE THREE MEN WHO WERE FINALLY BROUGHT TO TRIAL AND CONVICTED TURNED OUT TO BE INNOCENT VICTIMS OF A BLATANT MISCARRIAGE OF JUSTICE.

However, in the end, the dogged persistence of lawyers, political campaigners, and policemen determined to right the injustices of the past, ensured that the guilty man was eventually found – in a twist of fate that few could have predicted.

Stabbed over fifty times

It was in the early hours of St Valentine's Day that Lynette White, a young prostitute working in the docks area of Cardiff, brought her client to a shabby apartment over a betting shop. The electricity in the apartment had been cut off because the bill had not been paid, and the rooms were lit only by the street lights outside. At some point in the encounter, there was an argument over payment, the man demanding back the money that he had given White, and White refusing

Lynette White, a young prostitute, who was murdered in a frenzied attack in the docks area of Cardiff

to hand it over. It was hardly a great sum – only thirty pounds – but in the end, it cost White her life. Enraged, the man took a knife and stabbed White more than fifty times, slitting her throat from ear to ear and mutilating her body hideously. Most of the stab wounds were concentrated around her breasts, in a way that suggested the murderer was a deeply psychotic individual, who had suddenly become deranged to a frightening degree.

Naturally, the citizens of the docks area were horrified. The docklands part of Cardiff, once known as Tiger Bay, was a poor, run-down area of the city, but it was well known to have a close-knit, tolerant community – in fact, the oldest multiracial community in Britain, dating from the nineteenth century – in which the crime rate was surprisingly low. However, it was a part of town where petty lawbreaking was common enough, and there were inevitably tensions between the police and some local residents. When Lynette White was killed, the police immediately pointed the finger at three men – initially five – who had been a thorn in their side for many years.

Bloodstained white man

The first of these, Stephen Miller, had been Lynette White's pimp and boyfriend.

Unbeknown to him, he actually had an alibi, having been seen playing pool at a local pub very shortly after the murder – without a drop of blood on his clothes. This alibi came from statements to police that were made by other suspects and witnesses. (The time of the murder, at between 1.45 and 1.50 am, was known because White's watch had stopped, something that often happens when a wearer experiences intense shock.) Despite this knowledge, the police continued to press charges. Miller was of very low intelligence – he was later identified as having a mental age of eleven – and did not realize that he had an alibi for the time of the murder. Police managed to extract a confession out of him, which he later retracted. They then went on to charge four other local men who all protested their innocence: John Actie, Ronnie Actie, Tony Paris and Yusuf Abdullahi.

There were many anomalies in their statements, and the evidence against them was shaky to say the least. Some of the men charged had alibis for the time in question; Abdullahi, for example, was working aboard a ship at the time and had thirteen witnesses to prove it. Not only this, but other witnesses reported seeing a bloodstained white man in the vicinity of the apartment where White had been murdered – yet all of the men charged were black, or of mixed-race origin. But most significantly, the scientific evidence against the men was entirely lacking. The blood samples taken from the scene of the crime did not match those of any of the men charged.

Tony Paris (below) was one of the three men – known as the Cardiff Three – charged with murdering Lynette White. A mouth swab and subsequent DNA test proved his absolute innocence

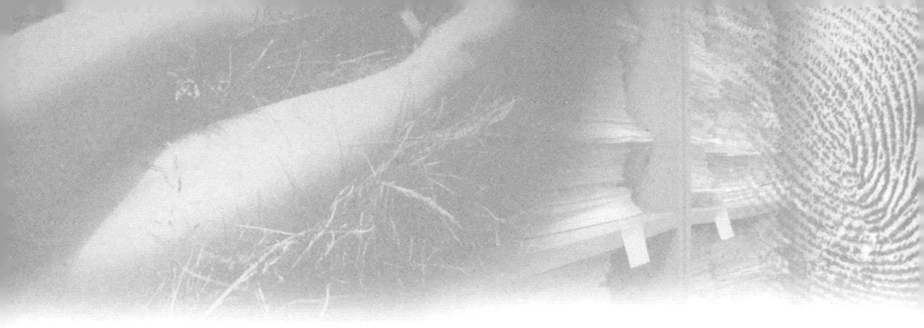

In order to explain this glaring anomaly, the police came up with a highly unlikely scenario: that the five men had been part of a larger group, all of whom had murdered Lynette White in an orgy of violence. According to the police, the blood found at the scene of the crime was that of one of the other men, who had somehow got away and had never been traced. (And who, moreover, could not be identified by any of the supposed co-murderers.) Unbelievably, the legal procedures that should have stopped this case ever coming to court failed to do so, and the police managed to bring the charges against the five men all the way to court. Even more unbelievably, the jury eventually convicted three of the men on the basis of this 'evidence': Miller, Paris, and Abdullahi. The other two men, cousins John and Ronnie Actie, were acquitted, for reasons that seemed equally obscure. To most onlookers, the case did not make sense, and was a travesty of justice.

'Cellophane Man'

Miller, Paris, and Abdullahi all received life sentences, and began to serve their time in jail. But the story was far from over. The media were in uproar, and 'the Cardiff Three', as they became known, found themselves at the centre of a campaign run by a small but tenacious group of supporters, including family members, political campaigners and legal practitioners. After a great deal of hard work, and an appeal through the law courts, the convictions were overturned, and the three were eventually released in December 1992. The Lord Chief Justice ruled that Stephen Miller's confession was unlawful and should never have been admitted as evidence. Yet although the supporters of the Cardiff Three were jubilant, all agreed that this was a sorry day for British justice, which had been shown to have wrongfully imprisoned three men for a crime they did not commit, in the process ruining their family lives, their psychological health, and their ability to earn a living. Moreover, many commentators accused the police of overt racism, since the three men convicted were all black or of mixed-race origin – even though the prime suspect had initially been a white man.

The Cardiff Three were finally free, having had their lives profoundly disrupted for several years, including four years serving time in jail. But police had got no further in finding the killer. However, in the years that followed, important advances were being made in DNA profiling. In 1998, a process became available so that tiny samples of blood, even down to one single cell, could be analysed. This meant that new evidence in the Lynette White case could now be put forward. New blood samples had been collected from the scene of the crime: from the cellophane of a cigarette package, and underneath paint on the wall of the room where the body had been found. The DNA on these samples was quite clear, and police knew that whoever matched up with it was the killer. The hunt for the 'Cellophane Man', as he now became known, was on.

Jeffrey Gafoor was tracked down thanks to good detective work and DNA profiling

By this time, many of the old guard of the police force had retired and incoming officers wanted to make a fresh start. A new unit was set up to investigate unsolved cases, and top priority was, of course, the infamous Lynette White case, still unsolved after more than a decade. The police now made it their business to bring White's killer to justice once and for all, thus drawing a line under the shameful episodes of the past.

With the help of tireless campaigner Satish Sekar, the police sifted through

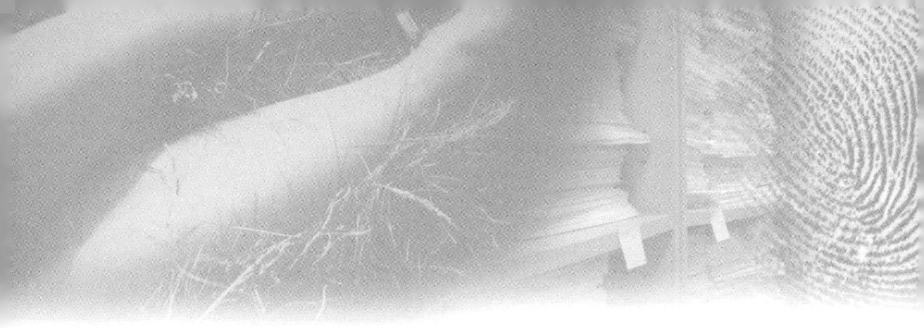

their DNA files again and again, until they came up with a close match to the blood sample left by 'Cellophane Man'. This was initially disappointing, as it came from a fourteen-year-old boy who could not have committed the murder since he was not even born at the time. The police then decided to take a look at some of the boy's relatives, whether they were known to the police or not.

A quiet loner

This line of inquiry soon led them to Jeffrey Gafoor, a security guard who had never been in trouble with the police before the murder was committed, and who had only once been convicted of a minor assault after it, for which he had done community service. Such an individual was, of course, an incredibly difficult person to find: but through the DNA profiling, the police caught up with him.

Described as a 'quiet loner', Gafoor lived on his own and had few friends. When the police interviewed him, he admitted having sex with White a week before the murder, and asked if his semen had been found on her. The police realized that Gafoor was trying to set up a story explaining the presence of his DNA at the scene of the crime. They were convinced that they had found their man, and when they left, after taking a sample from him, they put him under surveillance. Gafoor then took an overdose of paracetamol, but his attempt at suicide was interrupted when the police broke down his door. He was rushed to hospital, where he admitted that he had killed Lynette White.

When Gafoor recovered, he was brought to trial, pleaded guilty and was convicted of murder. In July 2003, he was sentenced to life imprisonment. This was the first time that the British courts had convicted a murderer after letting out the original convicted men on appeal. It was a triumph, not only for the campaigners who had continued to keep up the pressure after the Cardiff Three were released, but for the police, who had done their utmost to make up for the errors of the past, and this time find the real culprit. After fifteen years, justice was finally done and the killer of Lynette White was put behind bars.

MARION CROFTS: A GIRL TOO YOUNG TO DIE

MARION CROFTS WAS A TEENAGE GIRL WHO WAS BRUTALLY RAPED AND MURDERED IN THE UNITED KINGDOM IN 1981. POLICE MOUNTED A HUGE SEARCH FOR HER KILLER, QUESTIONING THOUSANDS OF LOCAL PEOPLE IN AND AROUND THE AREA OF FLEET, HAMPSHIRE, WHERE SHE LIVED. DESPITE THE ENORMOUS AMOUNT OF EFFORT PUT INTO FINDING HER KILLER, IT WAS ALL TO NO AVAIL, AND THE CRIME WENT UNSOLVED.

However, there was one thing that police did that was to prove crucially important. Samples of her body and clothing were taken from the scene of the crime for forensic analysis. Nothing very useful could be done with them at the time, but experts knew that in future years, the technology would become available whereby a microscopic DNA analysis could be made, showing the identity of the killer. Of course, a match would also have to be made between the DNA from the sample and the DNA of a criminal on the police's files, and no one could predict whether that would be possible. The chances of finding the perpetrator of the crime were slim, yet, all the same, the samples were filed away safely, just in case they should be needed in future. And twenty years later, the police's foresight, and their faith that one day the killer would be found, proved to be justified.

Raped, beaten, and strangled

Marion Crofts was just fourteen when she left her home to bicycle to a band practise at Wavell School in Farnborough. That was the last time anyone saw her. She was later found dead on the cycle route. She had been attacked beside some bushes near a canal towpath, and when her body was examined, it was found that she had been raped, beaten, and then strangled to death.

In 1981, police could do little with the forensics taken from the scene of the crime. These samples then revealed her killer twenty years later

The crime shocked the quiet, law-abiding community where she lived, and a massive murder investigation was launched by the local police. Thousands of men living in the area were asked to complete a questionnaire, and many of them were interviewed, but despite these efforts, no arrests were made. By 1983, the investigation had been scaled down and, to the dismay of Marion's family and friends, it looked as though her name would remain on the list of unsolved murders for the foreseeable future.

However, when the police had examined Marion's body at the scene of the crime, forensic experts had taken samples from the girl's clothing and transferred them to a laboratory microscope slide. This was filed away, in the hope that it would become useful once DNA profiling techniques became available in the future, so that the killer would be found. As it turned out, this is just what happened.

Bodily fluids

In 1999, police re-examined the Crofts case, extracting a full DNA profile from the sample on the slide. The profile was then checked against the national DNA database held by police, which contained DNA samples from all known criminals in the country. This was a laborious task, which was performed repeatedly in the hopes of yielding some new information on Marion's killer, but for a long time no match was made and it looked as though the mystery would never be solved.

Not deterred, the police regularly checked and updated the information, and two years later, in August 2001, their perseverance paid off. A match was made between the sample and bodily fluids from a man named Tony Jasinskyj.

Jasinskyj had been picked up by police for assaulting his second wife, who had accused him of beating her. Before he left police custody, a mouth swab had been taken for DNA analysis and the results had been routinely loaded into the database. To the astonishment and delight of the researchers, there was a match

Marion's bicycle was found on a road near her house. She had been dragged to a canal towpath where she was raped, beaten and killed

The profile was then checked against the national DNA database held by police, which contained DNA examples from all known criminals in the country.

between his profile and the Crofts sample from 1981, and police immediately brought Jasinskyj in for questioning.

Jasinskyj was by now aged forty-five. It emerged that he had been working as a cook in the local army barracks at the time of the Crofts murder and that, in fact, he had been one of the thousands of men who had filled out a police questionnaire as to his whereabouts at the time. On the form, he had claimed to be at work at the time the teenager was killed, and had maintained that he had never been anywhere near the spot where her body was found.

'A nice guy'

Since 1981, Jasinskyj had left the army and was now working night shifts as a security guard in the town of Leicester. After the assault on his wife, he had been banned from visiting his children at home, and had temporarily become homeless, so a former colleague had helped him out by having him to stay for a few days. The colleague described him as a kind, helpful person, and described how he had been an easy house guest. Most of the time, he said, Jasinskyj had been out at work; when he was in the house he had spent most of his time sleeping, smoking, eating bowls of Cheerios, and playing the guitar. Jasinskyj had spoken about his wife and children a great deal, and told his friend how much he

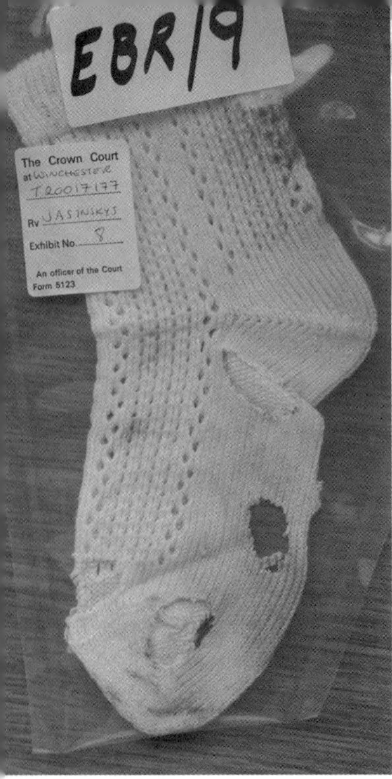

One of Marion Crofts' socks which she was wearing when she was murdered. A DNA profile was constructed from her clothing in 1999

was missing them. 'He was the nicest guy you could ever meet,' said the friend. 'He would do anything to help anybody.' On hearing that Jasinskyj was a murderer his friend was astounded, commenting, 'I feel like a bad judge of character.'

Brought to justice

In 2001, Jasinskyj was arrested for the rape and murder of Marion Crofts. The following year he was brought to trial and was convicted. He was given a life sentence. The DNA evidence was, of course, crucial to the case. It was essential to establish that the sample on the microscope slide was the right one, that it had been filed correctly and that no errors had been made in maintaining the files – after all, a man's freedom was at stake. The defence, not surprisingly, were keen to show that such an old sample could easily have been wrongly labelled or tampered with, but it appeared that the police forensic service had catalogued the results meticulously. As a forensic expert stated, on record, at the time: 'The Forensic Science Service made a decision to put things on hold as far as the slide was concerned – and it effectively became a time capsule.' He went on to explain that the slide sample had been untouched in 1981, for fear of damaging the DNA cells on it. He continued, 'We retained the evidence well and every time we looked at anything it was noted properly. We even knew who prepared the original laboratory slide and this scientist was able to give evidence confirming that this was the microscope slide prepared in 1981.'

Summing up, the judge at Winchester Crown Court praised the work of the Forensic Science Service. Marion's family also personally thanked the police officers involved in the case.

Thus it was that the tragic case of Marion Crofts, a young girl who had everything to live for and whose life was brutally cut short when she was only fourteen years old, was finally solved. It had taken over twenty years to bring her killer to justice, and had it not been for advances in DNA profiling technology, the chances of ever tracking him down would have been very remote. As it was, the police forensic department's forethought in taking samples from her clothing, at a time when the technology for DNA analysis was still in its infancy, made it possible to conduct a thorough check at a later date. Not only this, but the careful way in which the microscope slide was maintained for more than two decades, untouched until the case was re-examined, meant that the evidence to convict the killer was extremely persuasive. There were those who argued that, over the passage of time, there might have been errors, but the police were able to produce full records to show that the sample was the right one. Had this not been the case, Marion Crofts' murder might, to this day, still appear on the United Kingdom's list of unsolved murder cases. As it was, the solving of the case was a triumph for the police and for Marion's family, who could now grieve in peace, knowing that the man who had killed their daughter had finally been brought to justice.

The DNA evidence was... crucial to the case...the slide sample had been untouched in 1981, for fear of damaging the DNA cells on it.

NANINE GRIMES: JUSTICE AFTER TWENTY-FIVE YEARS

IN RECENT YEARS, MANY COLD CASES HAVE BEEN SOLVED AFTER DECADES BY MATCHING DNA SAMPLES FROM THE SCENE OF THE CRIME WITH THAT OF CRIMINALS LISTED ON POLICE FILES. ADVANCES IN FORENSIC SCIENCE HAVE MEANT THAT VERY SMALL PIECES OF EVIDENCE THAT ARE TWENTY, THIRTY OR MORE YEARS OLD CAN NOW BE ANALYSED TO FIND THE PRESENCE OF DNA.

Police records have also been expanded and improved, so that now all convicted felons are listed on a database, with detailed information that includes their DNA profile. Sometimes these felons will have been picked up for very minor offences that may have nothing whatsoever to do with murder. But now, with computer technology, it is a relatively simple job to sift through the thousands of DNA profiles on the databases and match them up with a DNA sample from the scene of a crime.

Of course, in some cases, a murderer will not appear on the database, simply because he or she has not committed a felony since the killing; however, in most cases someone who has committed a major crime tends to continue to disobey the law, even if only in minor ways. In this way, a killer may indeed think they have got away with murder, and may sometimes walk free for many years, but they will

A vastly improved database linking police forces in the UK means that police can now match up a DNA profile – among other forms of identity, too – with a DNA sample found at the scene of the crime

eventually appear on a database, perhaps for forging a signature, or giving a false address, or some such small infraction of the law. Thus, ironically, through committing a minor felony they will be tracked down and charged with murder, after years of thinking that their brutal crime has been forgotten for good.

Eighty stab wounds

One of the most dramatic such cases was that of Nanine Grimes, a fifteen-year-old schoolgirl who was murdered in the bedroom of her home in Adams County, Colorado, on 4 September 1980. She was found mutilated and covered in blood on her bed by her older sister, Deanna. Nanine was small in stature, but evidence showed that she had put up a brave fight against her attacker, since the man who killed her had bled copiously over his victim, and over the headboard of the bed where the murder took place. The evidence also showed that this had been a horrifying, frenzied attack: there were more than eighty stab wounds on Nanine's body.

Another sad aspect to cold cases: Troy Brownlow had decided to 'go straight'; he had settled down into a new job and was about to become a father when the crime he committed twenty-five years before re-emerged – and demanded justice

This brutal murder of a teenage girl traumatized the local community, but despite the efforts of the police, it took twenty-five years to track down a suspect for the murder. In April 2005, forty-two-year-old Troy Brownlow was arrested at a convenience store in Tucson, Arizona, and taken into police custody. At the time of his arrest, Brownlow was working as a personal trainer at a fitness centre, but he had a history of brushes with the law, and his DNA profile had been put on a database after his release from an Arizona prison. Incredibly, Brownlow's DNA

Nanine was small in stature, but...she had put up a brave fight against her attacker, since the man who killed her had bled copiously over his victim.

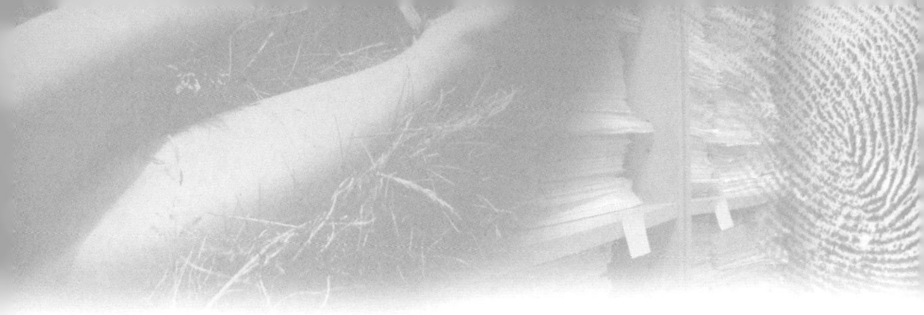

He had also been an acquaintance of Nanine's sister, Deanna...she had known him since third grade, and... they had graduated from Thornton High School together in 1982.

profile matched that of blood samples taken from the scene of the crime where Nanine Grimes was murdered in 1982.

Drug and alcohol abuse

It turned out that Brownlow, now living in Tucson, had indeed been a neighbour of Nanine's in Adams County all those years ago. In fact, he had lived less than half a mile away from the Grimes' house. He had also been an acquaintance of Nanine's sister, Deanna. When told that Brownlow had been picked up as a suspect, Deanna Grimes commented that she had known him since third grade, and that they had graduated from Thornton High School together in 1982.

Since his schooldays, Brownlow had been in trouble with the law on numerous occasions. He had a long history of drug and alcohol abuse, and had spent two years in prison in Arizona after being convicted of burglary. He had also spent time in jail in Arapahoe County for firing a bullet at the house of an ex-lover. His adult life had for many years been in chaos, but at the time of his arrest he insisted that he was trying to go straight. During his last spell in jail, he had spent his time

quietly, reading, playing cards, and writing poetry. On being released, he had settled down in Tucson with his girlfriend, got a job as a personal trainer, and was looking forward to becoming a father.

White handkerchief a 'calling card'

In April 2005, Brownlow was charged with the murder of Nanine Grimes. There was some controversy over this, since he had been a juvenile at the time of the murder, but as many pointed out, since then he had had plenty of time as an adult to come forward and declare himself. However, when he was charged, Brownlow argued that although he had been present at the murder, he had not committed it.

In his own version of the story Brownlow said that he had been at the house several times with two of his schoolmates who were 'smitten' with Deanna, although he himself was not. On the afternoon of Nanine's death, he was out walking near the Grimes' house, and somehow got 'sucked into' the events that took place, though he would not explain how. While he was at the house, a big man, unknown to him, appeared. Brownlow described the stranger as 'a rough and tumble kind of guy' and 'a good-sized dude'. He then told how he had become frightened and run out of the back door, jumping over the fence and cutting himself as he did.

Brownlow was charged with murder. There was some controversy over this, since he had been a juvenile at the time of the murder.

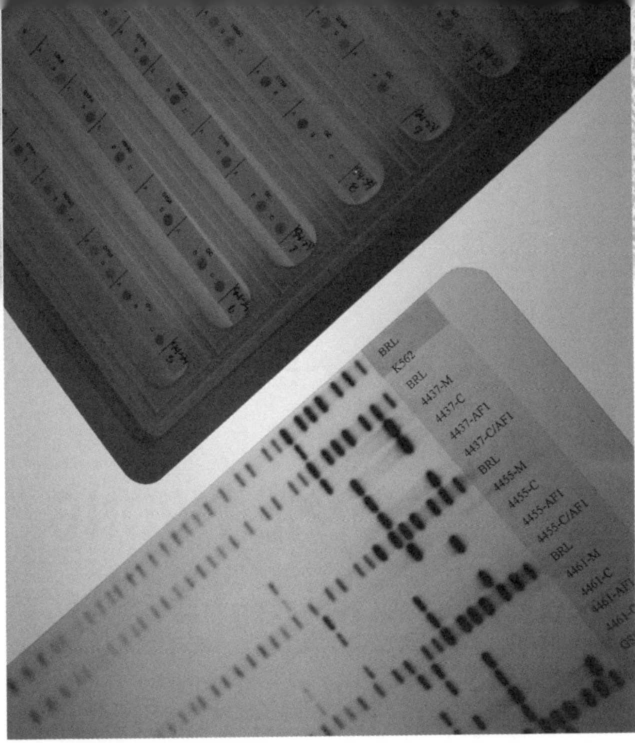

DNA mapping: forensic science is now sufficiently advanced that tiny pieces of evidence can be analysed for the presence of DNA many years after the crime has been committed

Expressing his remorse Brownlow went on to say that he had felt guilty about not reporting the crime ever since it happened. On one occasion, he had mentioned it to a friend over the telephone when he was in jail. He claimed that he bitterly regretted not having contacted the police at the time, or since, to come forward as a witness, but said that he had been afraid to do so. He said that he wished he could have apologized to Deanna Grimes 'for being a coward'. He also claimed that he had tried to stop the murder but failed.

Brownlow pointed out several anomalies in the case, such as the fact that the mattress from the bed had gone missing since the murder. He also alluded to the fact that, according to police reports, the murderer had placed a white handkerchief on the body as a kind of 'calling card', and that later, a 'taunting letter' had been sent to police. This indicated, he said, that a cold-blooded murderer had done the deed, not an inexperienced, frightened high school boy such as he was at the time.

Nevertheless, Brownlow was charged with murder and sent to trial.

JANE MIXER: THEY GOT THE WRONG MAN

IN MOST CASES, FORENSIC DNA TESTING YIELDS RESULTS THAT PROVE THE IDENTITY OF A KILLER BEYOND DOUBT. BUT JUST OCCASIONALLY, DNA RESULTS ADD TO THE MYSTERY OF A CRIME. THUS IT WAS WITH THE CASE OF JANE MIXER, A YOUNG LAW STUDENT WHO WAS MURDERED IN 1969, AND WHOSE KILLER CAME TO TRIAL THIRTY-SIX YEARS LATER.

In 1969, Jane Mixer was a young law student at the University of Michigan. She had recently got engaged and in March that year was due to head back home for the spring break. She posted a message on a bulletin board at the university and received the offer of a lift from a young man who she assumed was another student. According to friends, she did not seem to be worried about taking a ride across the country with a male stranger, but was more concerned with how her parents would take the news of her recent engagement.

Dumped in cemetery

On 20 March, Mixer's body was found dumped in a cemetery. She been shot at point-blank range in the head. She had also been strangled with a pair of pantyhose. Her naked body was exposed, but she had not been raped.

The scene of one of John Norman Collins' killings: the area where thirteen-year-old Kawn Basom was found. She was the fifth victim of Collins

At the time, there had been a spate of around half a dozen murders in and around the university, all of them young women. Mixer's murder was believed to be the work of the same killer, even though there were significant differences between her killing and that of the others: for instance, the others were not shot, and in most cases their bodies had been hidden away in bushes or under trees, rather than laid out in the open. Even so, Mixer's murder was put down to this serial killer, and eventually police tracked down the man they believed to be the culprit. John Norman Collins was arrested in 1970, accused of the murders, and convicted. He was sentenced to life in prison.

For many years, it was believed that the Mixer murder had been solved, but there were those who had their doubts. Over three decades later, the case was reopened and re-investigated. This time, DNA tests showed that the stains on Mixer's pantyhose linked to Gary Leiterman, a retired nurse now in his early sixties, whose name was in a felon's database because he had pleaded guilty to forging prescriptions.

The mystery blood spot

When detectives investigated further, they found that at the time of Mixer's murder, Leiterman had been twenty-five years old and working as a drug

When Collins was imprisoned for his series of murders in and around Michigan University, it was assumed that he had killed Jane Mixer. When the case was re-opened in the late 1990s, this was found not to be true

salesman. He had lived about half an hour from Mixer's dormitory building, and had owned the same type of gun that had killed Mixer. Most tellingly, he had bragged to his room-mate that he was capable of rendering a woman unconscious or even killing her with the powerful drugs he had at his disposal.

However, as well as Leiterman's DNA, the analysis turned up another piece of evidence that was completely mystifying. A spot of blood on the body's hand, which had been flaked off and saved as evidence by a police officer, turned out to have the DNA of another, different man.

To the excitement of the detectives on the case, it turned out that the DNA belonged to John Ruelas, a convicted murder now held in prison. Ruelas was the son of an abusive mother who had made his life a misery. He had eventually taken his revenge and murdered her, and was now serving a life sentence. He seemed exactly the sort of person who would have murdered Mixer. But then came the bad news: Ruelas was only forty years old now, and he was much too young to have committed the murder. At the time of Mixer's killing, he would have been just four.

There were several explanations for the findings, although none of them were

very satisfactory. First, it was thought that the evidence could have been contaminated. However, it was hard to explain exactly how a person could have contaminated evidence so as to show up Ruelas' DNA. Second, doubts were raised as to how accurate DNA testing actually was in this case – or, indeed, any case. Scientists maintained that the testing was one hundred per cent reliable, but if that was so, how could it have come about that a four-year-old boy had been responsible for the crime? It simply was not possible.

For Leiterman and his lawyers, of course, the new evidence was a godsend. They argued that Leiterman was innocent, and that the evidence had been contaminated in the laboratory. They also argued that the murder had been committed by John Norman Collins, the serial killer who had been tried and convicted in 1970 for the Michigan murders.

Surprise twist

However, the jury in the Leiterman case was not convinced. Despite the mystery of John Ruelas' DNA, they ended up convicting Leiterman, who received a life sentence. But there were many who disagreed, and who believed that Leiterman was innocent – or if not innocent, certainly not proved guilty.

The surprise twist in the Jane Mixer case, leading to the identification of a four-year-old boy as a murder suspect, has led many to question the infallibility of DNA testing. It has also led to speculation that the boy might have been present at the murder, although Ruelas denies this. It is perhaps possible that Ruelas could have been unknowingly involved in the murder in some way: he had had a chaotic childhood, and his mother had been involved with numerous drifters. Even so, it does seem unlikely that he was present at the scene of the crime.

Whatever the truth of the matter, it appears that in the Mixer case, DNA results were used to convict one man – Gary Leiterman – but ignored in the case of another – John Ruelas. The mystery of how a four-year-old boy's blood came to be on the body of murder victim Jane Mixer still remains.

ROSE TWELLS: A GUILTY CONSCIENCE BREAKS

IN A SURPRISE TWIST, ONE OF THE OLDEST, COLDEST CASES IN UNITED STATES LEGAL HISTORY WAS SOLVED RECENTLY WHEN A MURDERER WAS FINALLY CONVICTED OF HIS CRIME, A FULL TWENTY-SIX YEARS AFTER THE EVENT.

At the time, the brutal murder he committed had rocked the close-knit community in which it took place; but as the years passed and the case was filed away as unsolved, it seemed eventually to be forgotten by all but the victim's family and close friends. However, there was one person, the murderer's former girlfriend, who did not forget, and finally had the courage to tell what she had seen: and it was her evidence that began to warm the case up once more, so that finally the murderer was retried, and this time, convicted.

Beaten to death

Eighty-six-year-old Rose Twells lived in a large, imposing house in Woodbury, New Jersey. She was the widow of the former mayor of the town, and well known to local people. One night, on 20 December 1979, her peaceful, pleasant way of life came to an end. Intruders came into her house, dragged her to the staircase, tied her to it, and beat her to death with an iron pot.

The murder looked as though it could have been the results of a botched

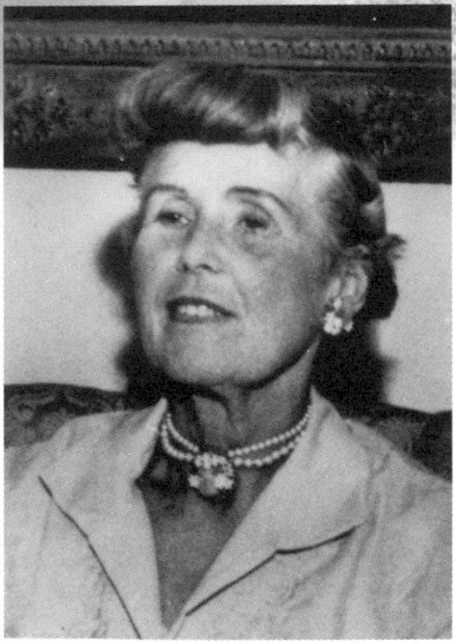

Rose Twells: a wealthy woman who attracted the attention of a teen gone bad

robbery, in which the thieves panicked and killed the owner of the house. Suspicion soon fell on the town troublemaker, Jeffrey Bayer, a surly, unmanageable teenager of sixteen. Jeffrey was the son of the town's mayor, Frederick Bayer, and had been a source of great embarrassment to his father with his wild, unruly behaviour. However, the violence of this crime was of a very different order to any of Jeffrey's previous escapades, and it seemed unlikely to the local police that he could have committed such a heinous crime.

However, eight days after the murder, young Bayer was brought in for questioning and asked to take a lie detector test. According to the police, he passed the test. No evidence linking him to the crime was found at Rose Twells' mansion, and the police were unable to find any clues that might suggest that Bayer was responsible for the murder. Without any other leads, the case began to go cold, and once the fuss about the murder had died down, it was filed away as unsolved.

Stealing a diamond ring

For many years, the Twells case was forgotten until a woman named Luanne Waller approached the police in 1993. Waller told them that she had been Bayer's girlfriend at the time of the murder, and that she had actually been involved in it. According to her story, she had acted as a look-out, waiting outside the mansion while Bayer went inside to commit the murder. Waller asked the police to grant her immunity from prosecution before testifying against Bayer, which was

From left to right, Mark English, Clifford Jeffrey and Jeffrey Bayer. English was acquitted of the charge of felony murder, but Jeffrey Bayer and Clifford Jeffrey were found guilty and are serving 30- and 12-year sentences in jail respectively

eventually agreed, although it took many years to grant and further slowed down the proceedings.

Waller went on to tell how Bayer planned the robbery of Twells' mansion with two friends of his, Clifford Jeffrey and Mark English. Bayer had noticed that Twells wore a ten-carat diamond ring, and was convinced that there would be other expensive items in the house for them to steal. Bayer also knew that the widow had entrusted his father Frederick with a key to the house. Bayer planned to steal the key and let himself and his friends into the house quietly one night.

Fear of reprisal

According to Waller, on the night of the robbery she herself remained outside the house and kept watch, while the three young men let themselves in. She did not see what happened next, but when they came out they told her in graphic detail. Apparently, Mark English had held Rose Twells down while Clifford Jeffrey had stolen her jewels and other valuables. Then Bayer had taken an iron pot and beaten the old lady to death with it.

Not surprisingly, Waller believed Bayer when he said that if she went to the police, he would kill her. For that reason, she had remained silent for many years, but now, her conscience had led her to come forward with the story.

Bayer, now aged forty-one, was arrested and charged with the murder. He

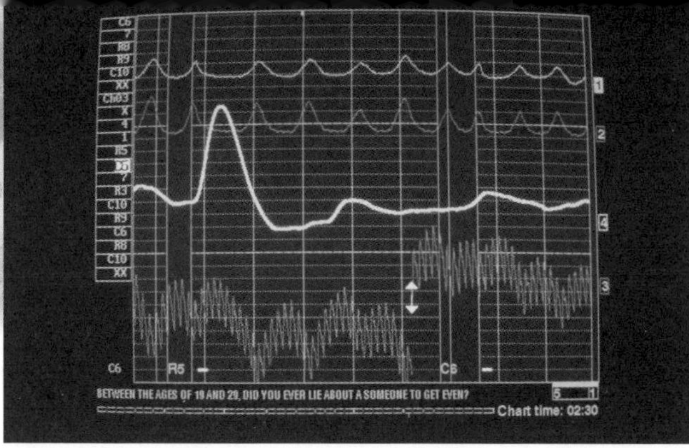

Lie detectors do not detect lies – they detect stress in the body by measuring the respiratory rate (top two lines), the sweatiness of the fingertips (middle line) and the blood pressure (bottom line). The question being asked at the time is stated too

claimed to have had nothing to do with it. But by now, he had acquired a criminal record. Over the years, he had been in trouble with the law on numerous occasions, for robbery among other crimes. However, even though Bayer's record implied he was the kind of person who could well commit such a crime, there was still no actual physical evidence linking him to it, a fact which made it difficult to pin the murder on him.

Bragged about murder

Then another witness stepped forward. This was Shirley Logan, who at the time had been Clifford Jeffrey's girlfriend. Logan told how she had gone to a party a week after the murder took place and heard Bayer boasting to his friends about it. The police then tracked down other witnesses, including Bayer's former classmates, who told the same story: that he had boasted to them about murdering Rose Twells. And, apparently, as he continued his life of crime, Bayer had gone on bragging, this time to prison inmates who he had shared a cell with when he was imprisoned for his various felonies.

After much deliberation, the jury convicted Jeffrey Bayer of murder, based on the evidence of the witnesses. On 2005 he was sentenced to thirty years in prison. Clifford Jeffrey and Mark English were also charged with murder, and arrangements were made for them to be tried separately.

Once again, a murderer was brought to justice, long after the deed was committed. Bayer must have assumed, after so many years, that he had got away with his crime; yet, in a twist of fate that he did not foresee, the people he had boasted to about the murder of Rose Twells finally stepped forward and brought him his rightful punishment.

INDEX